OGOU

A journey into the Underworld

JO MAY

GOThIC IMAGE
P U B L I C A T I O N S

Gothic Image Publications
7 High Street, Glastonbury,
Somerset, BA6 9DP

Cover design by Peter Woodcock

Editorial service by Jim Nagel,
set in Acorn Monotype Bembo

Printed and bound in Great Britain by
WBC Book Manufacturers Ltd,
Bridgend, Mid-Glamorgan

ISBN 0 906362 34 2

Contents

For Roz, Hannah, Em, Jer, Joe, my family, and all my relations

Acknowledgements

Eileen Herzberg, Caitlin Matthews, Cesca Potter, and Alexandra Campbell for encouragement and guidance. Colin Wilson for enthusiasm and kind words. Frances Howard-Gordon of Gothic Image for the courage and faith to take it on, and Jim Nagel for editorial service.

And to all those who contributed directly or indirectly, especially: David Rose, Judy Rose, Anna Wayne, Rob and Siggi Bennett, Freda Williams, Claire Lucas, Cheryl Straffon, Ian Cooke, John Heron, Peter Reason, Nic Hale, Alan Bleakley, Craig Weatherhill, Gabriel Hawkes, Marliet Denie, Ria Font Freide, Dan Wilson, Ralph Losey, *Time Team*, and all the participants on workshops who have helped to keep the place special.

oreword

I met Jo May for the first time in the early 1980s. I was doing some research for a series of television programmes about the paranormal in the West Country, and had heard about the remarkable "fogou" at Rosemerryn, a few miles beyond Penzance. I rang Jo, who invited me to come and see for myself.

My wife Joy and I arrived about mid-afternoon, and found the place full of people—Jo was running it as a conference centre for the study of human potential.

I found Jo an impressive sort of person — sincere and gentle, and totally lacking in the kind of pretension that I had seen so often among "gurus" in California. He showed us around the old house and its grounds, and we went down through the fogou—a kind of underground tunnel that curves downward under a bank with carefully built walls of the kind seen in passage graves; not far from the entrance there is a chamber off on the left. Joy, who is a good dowser, produced her dowsing rod, and it reacted powerfully in the area of the fogou, confirming Jo's claim that it seemed to be situated on some "line of power."

Now before I go any further, and before some down-to-earth reader drops this book with an exclamation of disgust, let me explain how I came to accept this notion of "earth forces."

In 1969, I could have said honestly that I regarded the whole subject of "the occult" with deep scepticism. When an American publisher asked me to write a book about it, I approached the idea with my tongue in my cheek—in fact, I undertook the commission largely because I needed the money. But it only took a few weeks of research to make me aware that ghosts, poltergeists, ESP, precognition and "second sight" were as well authenticated as any scientific phenomenon, and could certainly not be dismissed as wishful thinking. The vast body of solid evidence was overwhelming.

It was after *The Occult* appeared in 1971 that a publisher asked me if I intended writing about ley lines. When I asked "What are ley lines?", he sent me John Michell's book *The View Over Atlantis*, which introduced me to the notion of streams of "earth force" that run across the landscape, and which are taken for granted in China, where they are called *feng shui*. One day, a dowser came to call on us, and persuaded us to try using his divining rod. I got no result at all, but my wife had no problem in picking up an underground water pipe.

Some time later, when another dowser friend accompanied us to the stone circle called the Merry Maidens — not far from Rosemerryn — he offered me his dowsing rod — two strips of whalebone out of an old corset, tied together with string at one end — and I shook my head. "I can't dowse." He asked me to show him how I held the rods, and I showed him — holding either end between finger and thumb. He shook his head. "No, you've got to put a twist on the ends, so it has a spring on it." He made me hold my forearms parallel to my chest, placed the ends of the rod in my hands, and made me twist my fingers outwards. Then he made me lower the rod parallel to the ground, and told me to approach one of the stones. To my astonishment, the rod twisted upwards in my hands, towards my chest. I thought I had done it accidentally by changing the pressure, and tried another stone. It happened again. I tried crossing the centre of the circle, and the force there was extremely powerful, making the rod rise upward so powerfully that there was no further room for doubt. After ten minutes, it was clear that the rod was responding to some unknown force in the ground as a voltmeter responds to an electric current. At a nearby circle called Boscawen-un, the force was even stronger.

Some time later, I was in Carnac, Brittany, and Joy and I

went into the passage tomb of St Michel, where the force seemed to be extremely strong. But I was feeling out of sorts that day — irritable and headachey — and we soon went back into town for a glass of wine. The next day, we visited the great menhirs, where the force was less impressive than I had expected. Finally, as we drove off, and passed a field with some smaller standing stones in it, Joy said that she would like to try there. We had to climb over a fence. As soon as I approached one of the stones, the rod twisted in my hand with a strength that startled me. And it was the same with all the stones.

The explanation, according to a book by Paul Devereux that we had with us, was that when many tourists visit standing stones, they "use up" the power.

Before we left that field, my headache had returned, and I suddenly realized that it was connected with the standing stones. Because no tourists ever stopped to photograph them, they were more "highly charged" than the menhirs. I was glad to get back into the car. There was a farm cottage in the centre of the field, and I was amazed that anyone could live there. Perhaps they had grown immune to the force.

Which was why, when I visited Rosemerryn, I had no doubt that the "earth force" really exists. Probably sites like Carnac and Stonehenge were chosen for stone age "temples" because the earth force is so powerful there—I suspect that the stones have been stuck in the earth like acupuncture needles, and that our remote ancestors somehow knew how to channel or make use of the force — perhaps for healing. It is also interesting to note that Christian churches are often built on old pagan sites, as if the builders recognized this force as sacred.

All this is a necessary preliminary to what Jo had to tell me. We sat in his lounge, and he described how he had bought the house in 1978 — in spite of the fact that its previous four owners had died prematurely. One old countryman had told him that the place was "bad."

Jo, it seemed, had started life as an actor, training with the Bristol Old Vic. In 1971, at the age of 27, he married, and decided to give up acting in favour of psychotherapy and groupwork. After another period at university, where he read psychology and philosophy, he became a research fellow in psychology at the University of Surrey. Then, one day, he decided to abandon academic life and the prospect of tenure, and move to Cornwall to grow his own vegetables. His professor tried hard to dissuade him, but admitted that he felt envious.

So, with his wife Angela and two daughters, he moved into Rosemerryn, supported his family by renting out the cottage, and began running a psychotherapy practice. And, as he tells in the present book, he found himself driven by an obsessive enthusiasm for the place — he hurled himself into rebuilding, and into turning the wilderness into a vegetable garden.

In his enthusiasm, he failed to realize that Angela was having to readjust to a new life, so that when things suddenly broke apart, he was shattered. No amount of work on the house could compensate for the loss of his wife and daughters.

He told us how one day, he was sitting in his armchair in the corner of the room, feeling torn apart by misery and confusion, when quite suddenly he found himself up in the air, looking down on his own body. Suddenly, he was seeing himself "from outside", as if he was looking at another person, and knew that this misery would pass. When, a few seconds later, he found himself back in his own body, the misery had evaporated, and he felt at peace.

He went on to explain to us that he felt Rosemerryn possessed some tremendous force that could be dangerous to those who were out of tune with it. The answer lay in being able to harmonize with this force, and to use it.

It seemed to me that what he was saying was of tremendous importance. In fact, he was voicing my own lifelong obsession. The starting point of my first book, *The Outsider*, had been the enormous number of talented artists, poets and thinkers of the 19th century who had committed suicide. They had caught glimpses of a state of intensity and inner freedom that made "the triviality of everydayness" seem unbearable. Yet it seemed to me that the real problem was weakness and self-pity, a tendency to give way to our emotions. Saints and ascetics had always experienced a sense of world-rejection, yet had not committed suicide. They had persisted, gone through the long and painful process of achieving some kind of self-control and self-knowledge, and ended by inspiring other human beings instead of turning into frustrated misfits.

Jo's experience of looking down on himself had obviously given him the same insight. Like my "Outsider", he found himself in the position of someone who had somehow subjected himself to a force greater than his personal self. Such a force can be dangerous and destructive, like the force of a fast-flowing river. Yet it can also be harnessed to drive a dynamo. And since I had sensed the presence of this force at Carnac, I recognized that it would be used for creative purposes. I admired Jo for recognizing this, and setting out to achieve it.

About two years ago, Jo sent me the typescript of this book. I read it and was enthusiastic. I was also interested to find out how much Jo had learned about the fogou since then.

When we were at Rosemerryn, he had mentioned that a "sensitive" had told him that the fogou had at some time been used for dubious occult practices, and that it had been necessary to "cleanse" it. Again, it had struck me as the kind of comment that would have been absurd to me in 1969 but that I could now accept as simply factual. The "earth force" seems to be capable of recording human emotions. Around the turn of the century Sir Oliver Lodge had theorized that "ghosts" may be some kind of recording, imprinted in the fabric of old buildings by the negative emotions of those who have lived — and perhaps died tragically — there. Tom Lethbridge, an extraordinary dowser who was also a Cambridge don with a passion for archaeology, came to suspect that fields of earth magnetism are capable of "recording" events and emotions. Dr

Arthur Guirdham, official consultant for the Bath medical area, told me of houses where there had been a series of suicides or mental illnesses, and said that he thought they had also come to house some negative influence. And Paul Devereux had once mentioned how, when he visited the Rollright Stones near Oxford, he found a dead kitten that had obviously been used in some witchcraft ceremony, and how it had taken several days to cleanse away the unpleasantness.

So I was not surprised to discover, from his book, that Jo had come to believe that he had learned something of the past history of the fogou, dating back to the Celts who had originally lived on the site.

On my initial reading, I was a little dubious when, with the second chapter, the book slips into a kind of fiction. It seemed to me that he had an important and interesting story to tell, and that by introducing this fictional element, he was raising an element of doubt in the reader's mind. But when I had finished the book, I could understand why he had decided to write five chapters in the form of fiction. It is the only way of conveying the immediacy of his sense of the past, his feeling that it is as real as the present.

Undoubtedly, Rosemerryn is a place of power, a place where some psychic energy forms a link between this world and some parallel region. I am not sure whether I would have been capable of living at Rosemerryn — any more than I would have been capable of living in that cottage in the middle of a field in Carnac. But I believe that, in living there and coming to terms with its forces, Jo has learned a profound truth about the nature of human existence: that if it is to be understood, it has to be lived at a level of energy that causes all our natural laziness to protest.

Fogou is a remarkable book by an extraordinary man.

Colin Wilson

*I*ntroduction

Beyond the walls of the old house and buried in a tangled mound of short tufted shrubs and undergrowth, is the mouth of a cave—or fogou as it is known in Cornish. The entrance, lipped with pillars of granite, nestles between two mossy banks, sucking life into its womb.

You feel drawn in.

It is a passage made by humankind, long, dark and narrow, slabbed with massive granite lintels, curving gently as it slides into the

Fogou entrance
(Claire Lucas)

earth. Inside, its walls are wet with the earth's juices, and the air is heavy with soil musk. Silence hugs you, squeezing out the sounds of the world with a gentle contraction. You stand still, sensing the earth's pulse, waiting.

Soil sweat drips from the massive lintels above your head. In the fast fading light you can see a bat flitting back and forth along the passageway.

Your heart pumps. Suppose it flies into your hair?

You retreat a couple of steps, then force yourself forwards just as the creature flies straight at you, lightly skimming your head.

The bat retreats into a crevice and darkness closes in. The only sounds are your breathing and heartbeat.

And then the voices come.

You want to cling to reality and block the voices out. But they are insistent, and you listen because although you hear them with your mind, they speak with a voice that is not your own. And locked in here for centuries, they want to be heard.

The Celts came first.

Refugees from Brittany, they beached their leather-sailed boats at Lamorna Cove, made their way up the valley beside the stream, and settled on a small promontory a mile inland. There they built their homestead, ringed with a stone-walled bank. In time it became a place of knowledge, linked with a network of similar sites at the Land's End. They were a courteous and civilized people, bonded by kinship, and they stayed preserving their cultural tradition throughout the Roman occupation, leaving only when the Saxons came.

Two thousand years later, you can still see the remains of the fortified settlement and feel the presence of those people. Traces remain in the landscape of the mysterious network of stones and ancient sites, and people from the twentieth century are reawakening to their meaning and power.

The fogou is located at the head of the Lamorna Valley, near Land's End on the site of a three-acre Iron Age fortified settlement.[1] An oval ring of defensive works and embankment would have protected it in times of danger. The occupants of the fort were protected by a chieftain. I shall call him "Clwydd".

Clwydd's people, and the local community, used the fogou as their spiritual centre for ceremony, initiation and teaching. Birth and death rituals were conducted in it, a transition zone between this world and the next. It may also have been used for initiations involving entombment, the initiate being sealed in for a time to face the underworld in order to overcome fear and so emerge "reborn". It was never used for burial. The whole site was considered a sacred space and its oval defences were perhaps raised not so much to keep invaders out as to keep certain forces in. The place still has the feel of a world apart.

Clwydd's descendants left the fort to return to Brittany some time after the Romans went. The Romans themselves had left them alone, seldom travelling this far west, their nearest centre being Exeter. With the Romans' departure, Saxon invaders in the east began driving refugees westwards, and Irish Celtic raiders also created trouble.

The Celts, or at least their keepers of wisdom, the Druids, may have held keys to knowledge which could benefit us today. But as they never left anything in writing, we shall never know what they knew. Living in this land of theirs we can only learn again, our way.

In AD 937 the fields surrounding the site witnessed the slaughter of the last of the Cornish Celts led by Howel in their final battle against King Athelstan and his invading Saxon army. The fogou is known as the "Boleigh fogou", and "Boleigh" means "place of slaughter". Legend has it that after the battle the stream by the fort ran red with blood.

Jo May
1996

Celtic sword (Early Iron Age Antiquities, British Museum, 1925)

I

The Curse

I bought the place from a widow.

A short while after she and her husband, a botanist, first arrived, she had a premonition about an expedition he was about to make, and tried to persuade him not to go. A few days later, in Norway seeking plants for his collection, his car was hit by a train and he was killed. She stayed on looking after the place as best she could, but the signs of neglect were beginning to show.

On our first inspection of the property, my wife, Angela, and I were captivated. I knew I had to live here, even before I had seen inside the house. In retrospect, it was as if something on the land tapped me on the shoulder and said, "You'll do." The place grabbed me.

I had rejected a potentially fruitful career as a university psychologist in favour of moving to the country with Angela and our two young children, to be self-sufficient and to establish a centre where I could work with people. I had nagging premonitions about the impending collapse of society and wanted to establish an ark. I had also been heavily involved in the "growth movement", trying to "sort myself out", and now wanted to give something back.

The place wrought its magic on me and I became obsessed with learning new skills so I could minister to it. The grounds were a shambles and the house needed serious attention. I rewired, rebuilt, insulated, plumbed, plastered, chain-sawed, hacked and rotovated. By our second year I was growing all our vegetables, milking goats, getting stung by bees, raising chickens, cursing the fox, and even had my photo taken by passing Americans as I was scything hay.

It was as if the place was pushing me, pushing my usual pattern of driving myself obsessively. I would sometimes catch myself running from one job to another, my feet barely touching the ground, head thrust forward like Basil Fawlty, driven by the thought of what I had to do next. I was blind to Angela's struggling to cope with our two young children, but the land was responsive, almost as if it liked the attention that it was getting, and that I could have been giving her.

"You wouldn't catch me living in that house."

The old builder perched on the roof next door stopped spreading cement to gesture at Rosemerryn. A dying breed of craftsman, he was also the undertaker and wheelwright. "I wouldn't live there, boy, not if you paid me."

"Something to do with the fogou?" I asked, hoping to tap a rich vein of local wisdom.

"No good, boy."

And that was all I got.

I was fascinated by the fogou and began digging into the library to find out what I could about the history of the fort site. More recent writings referred to the house's spooky reputation.

> Odd tales had gradually clustered about the house, thick as the wisteria that trailed around its windows. Built about fifty years ago, it had since been inhabited by several different families; it had come to be considered an unlucky house. ... Unexplained incidents were said to happen there; the five-barred gate that separated its drive from that of the next house was always found open in the morning, however securely it had been fastened the night before. A revolving bookcase in one of the living rooms would be seen to turn without the touch of human hand; and in one of the bedrooms a lady looking into her mirror one day was horrified to see, not the expected reflection of herself and her

furniture, but a mist forming within the "many dimensions" of the looking-glass and becoming denser every second. She did not wait for further materialization, but hurried away. A boy sitting for his portrait to a young painter who had borrowed the studio was overcome by a sudden chill gust, though doors and windows were closed.[2]

I was reminded of our first night at Rosemerryn. As we lay in bed we heard a woman's sad, slightly demented laughter coming, as if from a long way away, from one of the empty bedrooms. I put it down to a radio. Now I began to wonder. "Sudden chill gusts" in the studio did not surprise me, having just replaced a leaking skylight. But if the house had a reputation for "the unexplained" and was "no good", what had we really taken on?

The next-door neighbours provided more information. Their house had been built before Rosemerryn. They had seen the heathland cleared, the walls of the old fort knocked down to be incorporated into a garden, the granite carted from the quarry in Lamorna Cove and the comings and goings of several families. Dropping by one evening, they commented on the changed atmosphere of the place, saying that they always used to feel uncomfortable when visiting, but that something had now disappeared. Seeing my interest, they told me more.

They said there was a ghost that would float down the stream by the house which usually foretold an untimely death. Two children had drowned there when their father was away at the Crusades. Others had seen the ghost of a monk picking his way through the woods towards the old fort.

They went on to say how, many years previously, they had been minding the house while the owners were away, and for a bit of a lark, had decided to hold a ouija-board session one night in the kitchen. Their seance, and regard for the unknown, underwent a radical shift when the candles blew out and the glass shot across the table and shattered.

"They say there's a curse on the place and that the male heads of the house will die unnaturally. But we don't think you need to worry now. Whatever it was has gone. You must have been accepted."

I checked the deeds and made some inquiries. Of the four previous owners, three were men: Benjamin Leader—an artist, Crosbie Garstin—an author, and my predecessor.

All had died prematurely.

2

lwydd

A few weeks later we were given more information. A woman called Freda was renting the cottage that is part of the estate and stands by the main gate. We had done it up as a holiday cottage and it provided most of our income. One morning, shortly before she left, Freda came to the house, agitated.

"I have to tell you this. I don't know why and I hope you won't think I'm foolish or trying to draw attention to myself. I'm really a very practical, down-to-earth person, but sometimes I 'see' things as if there's a cinema screen in my head. I've picked things up before. I don't ask for it, it just comes and I have to pass it on or it bothers me."

Freda checked to see how we were responding, and continued.

"Last night a man came to me. He was from a long time ago, long before there was a house here. He said he lived here. He said he was like a ... " She searched for the right word. " ... Like a chief. He wore a kind of tunic and cloak, and on his feet he had leather or goatskin boots, very fine with thongs criss-crossed up his calves. He was a big man, strong—inside too, I felt. He said a circle protected this place, a ring, and that it must be kept pure. That was very important. Only truth can be allowed to stay here. It will not tolerate intruders. When he lived here, this was a place of knowledge. He said his name was Clwydd."

We assured her that we did not think she was mad, and I told her what I knew about the fort site.

"Ah, that explains it then." She looked relieved and

something seemed to slip away from her. "Good. I can go now."

Freda's message lingered with me. I reflected on how it might have been at the fort in the days of the Celts, and with the help of things people told me, the local library, and I like to think, the fogou, I began to assemble a story.

3

Celts

By squinting his eyes slightly and steadying his breathing, Clwydd could just make out subtle distinctions in the movements of the bird as it stood by the stream craning its head this way and that. The tiny movements gave him the precise direction of the attackers and the sudden flight of the bird came as no surprise.

"There!" he whispered to the man beside him behind the stone palisade, and they both saw the movement in the trees.

A sixth sense had told him there would be raiders. He had stood behind the rampart, looking across the valley, scanning the trees and clearings for signs of movement. But there had been none. Trusting the feeling in his body, the tingling of his skin and the persistent inner voice, he had nevertheless called out to a nearby hut. A stocky red-haired man had appeared at the entrance.

"Warn the women to prepare themselves. We're going to be busy."

Rhia sat by the hearth looking into the flames. She could hear the men outside preparing for the attack, ushering the children and womenfolk into the hiding place. Figures seemed to appear in the tongues of fire, warriors in their battle gear, brandishing shields and swords. A gust of wind through the open doorway fanned the flames and made them leap brighter. Man's time is come, she thought, and felt a deep sadness. He burns with his power and no longer has need for mystery. She threw a pot of earth on the hearth, damped the flames, and left the hut.

In the fogou the women sat silently holding hands, their backs against the stone walls, eyes closed and breathing gently in unison. Children nestled into their sides or on their laps. The underground hush soothed away fears for their menfolk, and an air of peace settled in the passage.

Rhia sensed the earth's heartbeat pulse with hers and her sisters, intensifying the darkness. Black shapes swirled behind her closed eyelids taking unidentifiable forms.

She waited. Slowly the familiar sensations came over her — a sinking into herself, her feet rooting into the earth, a feeling as if her body was elongating and a light pressure around her head. Although still bodily in the fogou, she felt herself travelling over a great distance through dark spaces and spinning rainbow lights, far off a woman's voice calling her name. Her attention stretched like a taut skin between the insistent summons and the earthy contact of the passage.

Then she let go, felt something release, and saw the slender figure of a woman sitting upright by a hearth in a settlement some distance away. Rhia felt herself to be looking down at the woman from a point near the apex of the thatched roof of her hut.

"Welcome ... " A voice, not her own, spoke with her inner voice. "Beloved sister ... "

Space contracted further and Rhia snapped off the roof and entered, mingling and conversing with, the spirit of her sister.

Clwydd stood with his kinsmen half hidden behind the inner gate. He watched the raiders scramble over the outer wall, some already heading off the startled cattle, but most heading up the hill. There were about thirty of them, probably another desperate gang forced this way by the invaders in the East. He sought the leader and found him, a big man with fur tunic, crossed belts and horned helmet, carrying a two-handed sword. Clwydd waited until all the raiders were well inside the outermost ring, then shoved open the heavy gate, and with his small band close at his heels, ran shouting down the slope.

The leader of the raiders could not believe his eyes. His men outnumbered those of this small hill fort nearly two to one. Even a simpleton could see that the defenders should be staying in their fort to repel an attack, and yet here they were rushing towards him as if this was a game. Well, there would be some blood-letting now. He adjusted his helmet, hefted his great sword, and pictured himself by a warm hearth, wedged between a Celtic woman's thighs.

The heavy iron blade of the raider's two-handed sword slid horizontally upwards past his startled eyes, up past the horned helmet, and juddered against the downstroke of the Celt's broadsword. Tiny slivers of metal sparked off as the swords clashed. The Celt's steel swung back in an outflanking arc and slicing back and up, nicked the point of his elbow, severing fur and skin, and continued to his neck.

The raider's eyes rolled downwards in amazement at the Celt's speed, his brain racing signals to his arms to change direction. Back down came his heavy two-hander to parry the cut. An instant later, a reflex jerked back his horned head, dislodging his helmet and sending it in a graceful backwards curve as the Celt's sword point whistled past his throat.

Caught off balance, the raider chief was an easy prey. Clwydd's sword continued its movement uninterrupted, curved round, down and up again in a flashing figure-of-eight, and completed its trajectory in a straight-line vertical descent aimed precisely at the centre of the raider's skull.

Iron clove bone, splitting the wild-eyed face open as neatly as a log. And for quite literally a split second, the bewildered raider thought he was simultaneously in two worlds.

Next day, the council elders took Clwydd and shut him in the inner passage of the cave, sealing the opening with a tight-fitting boulder. Inside it was grave-dark and they left him there to face his own shadows, naked and without food or water.

He scooped out a pit near the back of the cave in which to defecate, made a small depression in the dusty floor near the entrance contoured to fit his hip as he slept, and found a spot half-way along the passage where he could sit in reasonable comfort with his back against a curved boulder in the wall.

Exercise was more of a problem since there was no room to stand and the passage was no more than an arm's span in width. Still, he was used to extended fasting, and it was warm down there, if a little damp. He had no doubt that, physically at least, he could easily endure several days entombment.

But it was not the physical that disturbed him.

"How long will I have to stay down there?"

"As long as it takes." The elders had examined him critically as he had stood before them at the council fire.

"You are stubborn. It could take a long time."

"Remember ... you do this for the clan."

They said I must wait, not do anything, not escape the waiting.

Time passes ...

I could dig out, remove some stones from the end there, just enough to see the light, to know I could do it ...

A bat crawled out of a crevice in the wall, sniffed man's smell, and crawled back.

I need to do something, can't sit here watching my mind all the time, pain in my backside, drip drip off the roof, what are they doing out there in the fields where the crops are, working in the rows, her body curving against thin goatskin, her mouth on mine, her smell, oh Rhia I can't breathe in here ...

A droplet of moisture formed like a globule of dark blood on one of the granite lintels above his head, grew heavy, stretched away from its stone skin, and plummeted.

Slash down the side of my face like the dodged spear between my eyes it was coming, why am I getting jumpy there's nothing out there, NOTHING OUT THERE! ...

Wet bat's fur twitched against granite, wings flexed ...

I can beat this thing, I can beat anything, how dare you taunt me and then say no. I'll thrust and stab... Whose thoughts are these? Cernunnos, dark lord of the underworld, there, just on the other side of the wall he is, I must catch him and hold him and keep him prisoner even if he rots and stops my breath with the stink, something is stirring out there ...

A shape formed at the end of the passage prising itself out of the rock. It dragged itself forward on sharp claws, its soft body scraping against the wall. Behind it trailed dragon's fins and the reeking stench of putrid meat.

Clwydd sat frozen as it approached, heart banging, eyes staring, breath stopped. The shuffling halted directly in front of him. He waited facing rank breath and a fetid stench. Soft fur and a warm pad glanced against his calf and began to slide up his inner thigh.

Not this, oh not this ...

"I won't let you do this to me!" He screamed into the stench.

The creature backed off a fraction.

"See who I am!" He hit out. Empty air. He rubbed his eyes hard, straining to see through the blackness.

"Clwydd ... " A voice, female. He cocked his head, listening, not sure, could it be outside? "I'm tired now, you rave so."

"Don't go ... "

"I must. Your brothers and sisters need me too."

"But I need you!"

"Hush, lie still now."

"Don't leave me, Ma! Not now! Just a little longer!" He held out his arms. "I want you!" then dropped forwards howling, his belly pumping up sobs which became rage, and he beat the ground with his fists and head.

"No! I won't let you! I'll show you I'm worthy!"

He saw himself sword in hand, cutting, slashing, slimed

with blood, facing death again and again, winning approval, admiration, confirmation.

"Oh Great Mother," he moaned. "What am I trying to prove?" And he lay face down in the dirt sobbing himself to sleep.

Many demons later he opened his eyes and saw light on the ground. He caressed it gently and was filled with acceptance, acceptance of his darkness, acceptance of his people, understanding of their oneness and love for the Great Mother that nurtured them all.

He looked up and saw sunlight flooding in through the open entrance, got to his feet and hobbled out. In the main passage he stood slowly erect and, shielding his eyes from the searing light, steadied himself against the wall of the entrance, his hand resting on a carving there — the guardian of the underworld, the god of healing. And the elders, gathered near the entrance, honoured him as befitted an initiate.

There were piles of equipment everywhere. Pots, urns, vases, jars of preserves, buckets, shovels, hoes, ploughshares, spears, anvils, hammers, axes, looms, boxes and bundles. And by tomorrow there would be nothing left, for the whole camp was leaving.

Years had passed since Clwydd's initiation, and the world outside the fort was changing. Saxon invaders in the east were forcing more and more people to leave their homes and live as best they could. These were troubled times and the choice before the clan was simple. Either stay, struggling to preserve their culture and traditions against the increasing waves of refugees, or leave and peacefully consolidate them.

A core of the women objected on the grounds that this was a sacred spot whose power should be preserved, and that they had work to do here tending and honouring the body of the Great Mother. It was a strong argument, but the elders maintained that the temples across the water were on a scale which surpassed anything one could imagine, and the clan's contribution to work of greater power would be valued. Oracles were consulted and the results settled the matter.

The women separated from the others as dusk fell on the last day, and gathered in the fogou where they offered prayers to the Goddess and asked for guidance as to how to keep the circle sacred in their absence. The answer came in a shared vision. They left the fogou, joined together in the centre of the settlement, and began chanting. Heads turned and voices became silent as the women processed in a line towards the perimeter of the camp, calling to the elementals and nature spirits. They touched stones, spoke to the trees and plants, summoned the animals, birds and insects, crying, mourning and singing soft goodbyes.

As the procession moved slowly around the boundaries, unseen forces came alive in its wake with ethereal forms and floating luminescence.

"Guard the power here, great spirits. Keep it sacred. Be mirrors to those who invade you, to those who cannot see. Turn evil spirits against themselves and repel them with their own dark places."

The line of women coiled its spell and bound it tight, and even the silently watching men could see the swelling ring of light.

Iron Age pot (British Museum, 1925)

4

Quern

A quern stone — a round stone with a flattened top and bottom, used for grinding corn—had been resting on a trough in the garden ever since I came. It is the best-preserved relic of the old settlement. One night I brought it indoors and sat with it for a while. This is what it "said":

Woman with quern (Victor Ambrus, Time Team)

We left because our culture was decaying, because many were leaving to the great places across the water. Our men wished to leave. They wanted the power and the glory of the great places with the stones. We were not happy to go. Yes, it was difficult here, and getting more so, and there was much to be done. Over there we could see that we would be lost in that great world, a world of men. Here we were still strong, but the men would have it so and so we left.

A group of us women performed the ceremony here to guard the circle. I was the last to leave. We did it at twilight on the night before we were due to leave. The men were in the main hut, although they joined us before going. There was much to do, much equipment to gather to load in the boats down in the cove. We used carts. It was very sad to leave this place, but we women had no choice; our arguments were not sufficiently strong.

*We said **this** was a place of power. Why leave it and go where we would be among many? They said that it would be harder to stay here. There were too many outside influences now, and many also wished to leave. We women felt something was dying that should not die, but we could not argue. What they said was true.*

The day we left, several of the women kept a vigil at the place, those who were strongest against going — there were three of them. I joined them only to drag them away. The fogou looked beautiful, many flowers and reeds and gifts. Yes there were offerings in pots, urns, and a beautiful vase containing sacred meat and bones and herbs. There was also fine jewellery — an amulet of bronze, delicately carved. Filga left that. She felt strongest about the place and not wanting to leave it. She left it at the last moment. There was also the priest who agreed with us in a way, but also agreed with the men that we should go. The men just wanted to go, the decision having been made.

The night before we left, as I said, there was last-minute packing of tools and small items. Large items like the livestock oxen were sold. We could not take them. We took gold for them from our neighbours. We women also participated that night, but later gathered to do our ceremony.

We gathered in the fogou and prayed to the Earth Mother to keep the place, the circle, sacred. Then we went outside and gathered in the centre of the circle, chanting. Then we walked slowly around the whole circle calling to the spirits, touching the stones, and weeping. There were many presences with us. It was the last of the times when we would be together, we and the spirits of this place who knew and understood each other so well.

We walked around. I talked to the plants and the trees. We sang to the birds. It was like a wake—much crying and saying of goodbyes. We asked for remembrance to stay here. We asked that all the stones, plants, animals, water, and all the "elementals" and spirits remember the place and keep it sacred from outside intruders—to keep the circle and repel invaders, those who would not be part of the Great Mother, or who had forgotten Her. They would work on the people who might come here to test them to see if they were living in truth with themselves and with the Mother. They would be very busy. They thought this was a good task. And so we left it so.

My name was not Rhia. It was Gaila. I worked the quern. You may call on me again if you wish.

5

agik

The seasons turned the wheel of the year. First the frosts and then the rains pitted out the remains of the clan's council fire. Around the perimeter of the fort, the undergrowth laid siege to the palisades. Roots tunnelled under the walls and creepers scaled them. Thick tendrils wrapped themselves around the remains of the huts and slowly, almost lovingly, fed on them and then pulled them down. The Great Mother reclaimed her gifts.

Centuries passed. The stone walls still stood, home now to the rabbits and birds, but little else. Human concerns had moved to distant parts of the land. Few came this way any more, and if they did, there was nothing to attract them into the wilderness. The earth kept its secret.

Except from one man.

Some time in the Middle Ages a lone figure dressed in a brown hooded robe teased his way through the thick brambles and bracken with his staff, attracted by a heron circling above the hill. Eager to escape the confines of his monastery, his nose had led him west to the old stone crosses and circles and standing stones, and now he stood looking up as the great white bird curled lazily around the hilltop.

The monk pushed past two elder bushes and almost bumped into the stone walls. Edging his way around, he found an entrance and entered the circle.

Silence settled like a meditation. He sensed the peace immediately. Some deep instinct made him inwardly thank the bird for showing him to this sanctuary, and he sat down, slipped out of his sandals, lay back and closed his eyes.

The humming of the bees and flying insects soon lulled him to sleep. Warmed by the sun and couched in soft grass, his sore muscles relaxed and he slid into the world of dreams.

A young woman dressed in flowing white with tiny folk dancing around her feet drifted towards him casting white rose petals on the ground around him. Some touched his body and turned into a cotton-like substance. The woman stopped by his head. Petals fell about his ears cocooning his head in fluff. He tasted its sweetness, and something seemed to drain away from him. Colours and sounds leaped out with startling freshness and clarity. Leaves sparkled like jewels. Streams of bees wove themselves in and out of the branches. A great moth settled at his feet and as it did so, the ground seemed to open up in front of him, the turves sliding back to reveal a deep pit with granite steps descending into wetness and another flight a little way beyond them ascending skywards, grey, then white, then dazzling gold.

He sat up, and the little figures, chattering gaily, fanned out gesturing to the pit, urging him either up or down. Looking into the blackness he felt pulled, sucked by the pit of his stomach. Ignoring his fear, he took two steps down then jumped across the gap to the steps which ascended. He began to climb. The air thinned and, looking back, he saw the little folk clustered around the woman in white, who seemed to be crying.

He paused, undecided as to whether to continue. The woman seemed to be beckoning him. He looked around to see if there was anyone else. But no. She meant him. She was imploring him to change direction. The way up seemed easy and strangely familiar. Yet somehow he felt that by choosing this way he was escaping.

Something about the woman touched him deeply. It was not her beauty, although that was striking. She seemed to radiate something that touched his heart. And as he gazed at her, her gaze met his, and for a moment everything shone.

He jumped, and his robe whisked off as he fell plunging back into the pit, the little white figures kaleidoscoping towards him in a chattering vortex. He plummeted down, skimming the descending steps, his naked body protected by a layer of slippery white fluid which streamed out behind him in a flickering tail. The figures, holding hands in a chain, caught the end and plunged after him.

He span gently, wide-eyed faces whirring before his, tongues licking him. Tiny hands clutched at him and began to pull him apart. Looking down at his belly he saw the skin stretch away and fingers of flame poking and wriggling out of the splits in his skin. His body tore into left and right halves, connected by a thick column of fire. Still the hands pulled, but now into a circle so that his two halves met.

As they touched, something exploded in his brain and he woke to the sun's glare and the humming of bees.

"You have been away for three whole days, Brother Michael, and have returned to us looking rather the worse for wear."

"Yes, Father."

"I should think that would merit some kind of an explanation."

"Yes, Father ... "

"Well?"

"It's very difficult. With all respect, Father, I doubt if you would understand."

"You must let me be the judge of that."

"Forgive me, Father. I have been feeling troubled of late and heard a call to go and seek my deliverance, which now, I believe I have found." Brother Michael, mud-smeared and tattered, radiated beatitude.

"Go on, Brother."

"There is an ancient place near the old stones which is full of wonders where I saw many things which lead me to consider if what we are doing is entirely the whole story."

"Oh yes?"

"We are led upwards, Father, in our quest for the divine, but there are also, surely, steps which lead down."

"Speak more clearly, Brother Michael."

"Going down we find our true selves, whereas going up we may be merely avoiding the knowledge of who we really are, which is, I know and do not doubt, true sons of God. But if God is within then perhaps we should seek him in here," Brother Michael pointed to his stomach, "instead of up there," he said, pointing to the ceiling.

"I see."

"There are many wonders that way," said Brother Michael, pointing to the floor.

"Undoubtedly you have made some startling discoveries in your absence from your duties, Brother, as your general appearance and expression would testify. I feel, however, that before we may benefit from the wisdom revealed by your experience, it would be best if you had a little rest."

Brother Michael was confined to his cell for a week and then set to work in the pig sties.

By the seventeenth century there was still standing

> the downfalls of a castle or treble entrenchment in the midst of which is a hole leading to a vault underground. How far it extends no man living now can tell, by reasons of the damps or thick vapours that are in it, for as soon as you go an arrow flight in it or less your candles will go out or extinguish themselves for want of air.[3]

Although known about locally and referred to as "the fuggo hole", many were afraid to enter it, even by day, as they believed it was inhabited by evil spirits.

> Women of villages near often threaten their crying babies that they will carry them down to the Fuggo and leave them there for the Bucca-Boo if they don't

20

stop their squalling, for it was believed to be haunted by beings of a fearful nature, whose path it was dangerous to cross.

The site became known as the Grambler Grove:

> well wooded, and the upper part thickly covered with hazel, thorn, and elder, with a tangled undergrowth of briars, brambles and furze. Few persons liked to pass this place, because strange noises were heard and fires often seen within it by night, when no one would venture near the place.[4]

By contrast, the surrounding valley and slopes had, since the thirteenth century, been a charming garden to the old mansion of Trove, with terraced walks, orchards, vines, pavilions, fish ponds, apiaries, herbs, vegetables, sunny banks of flowers, towering ornamental pigeonaries, artificial rabbit warrens, swans and a bowling green. This was the home of the Levellis family, who feature in a Cornish version of the Rumpelstiltskin story, "Duffy and the Devil".

Duffy, procured from the nearby village of St Buryan by Squire Levellis to weave and spin for him, forms a pact with a devil who offers to do her work if she will go away with him. Her only escape is to find out the devil's name.

A local witch, Bet of the Mill, offers to help Duffy. Disguising herself as a hare, she leads the squire and his hounds one night to the Grambler Grove, where the devil meets with a coven of witches.

> For miles we chased her—the finest hare that ever was seen, most in the dogs' mouths all the way, yet they couldn't catch her at all. Then we lost all sight and scent of her, till, tearing through brambles and thorns, we found ourselves in the Grambler Grove.
>
> And now I know for certain that what the old folks say is true—how witches meet the Devil there of summers' nights. In winter they assemble in the Fuggo

Hole, we all know, because one may often hear the devil piping for their dance. And now I believe that what we took for a hare was a witch that we chased into this haunted wood.

Looking through the thickets I spied, on a bare spot, surrounded by withered oaks, a glimmering flame rising through clouds of smoke. The dogs skulked back and stood around me like things scared. Getting nearer, and looking through an opening, I saw scores of women — some old and ugly, others young and pass-able enough as far as looks go. Most of them were busy gathering withered ferns or dry sticks for the fire. I noted too that other witches, if one might judge by their dress, were constantly arriving — flying in over the trees, some mounted on ragworts, brooms, ladles,

The Devil and Old Bet (Blight/Bottrell, 1873)

furze-pikes, or anything they could get astride of. Others came on through the smoke as comfortable as you please, sitting on three-legged stools and alighted by the fire, with their black cats on their laps. Many came in through the thickets like hares, made a spring through the flame, and came out of it as decent lasses as one might see.

A good large bonfire soon blazed up; then by its light I saw the old witch Bet of the Mill. And by her side a strapping dark-faced fellow that one wouldn't take to be a devil at all but for the company he was with, and the sight of his forked tail that just peeped out from under his coat skirts.

The devil got drunk at last and the witches, locked hand in hand, danced round the fire with him in their midst, singing: "By night and day, we will dance and play, with our noble captain, Tarraway! Tarraway!"

They danced madder and faster, pulled each other right through the fire, and they weren't so much as singed, the bitches. I wanted to dance with them and called out: "Hurrah! my merry devil and witches all!" In an instant, quick as lightning, the music stopped, out went the fire, a blast of wind swept away the embers and ashes, a cloud of dust and fire came in my eyes and nearly blinded me. When I again looked up they all had vanished.[5]

Another account of the same story told how the squire chased a witch for more than a mile through the fogou, owls and bats flapping around his head, his dogs fleeing terrified, foaming at the mouth. In the bowels of the fogou he saw scores of witches who had come from far and wide, some from as far as Wales astride enormous leeks. The devil and the witches "blew up" a fire and then danced "like the wind", the devil dancing in and out of the fire, giving the witches a "sound kicking".[6] Kicking, here, is a Victorian euphemism for

Witch (Hunt, 1871)

a "coarser word"—an allusion, perhaps, to the fogou's use as a venue for sex magic.[7] The parish of St Buryan has a rich folklore of witchcraft and tales such as these showed that the site had been a major site for "black" gatherings.

Aysha was an American woman who had psychic abilities. I knew of her under her previous name—Wendy Love—as the founder of Quaesitor, one of the first Growth Centres in Europe. Soon after Freda, the woman who told me about

Clwyyd, had left, Aysha had stopped by to see the fogou, which is mentioned in several guide books.

Aysha stood in the main passage, eyes closed, arms outstretched, breathing deeply—more for inspiration than lack of breath.

"Something terrible happened here. It needs clearing," she said with authority. "There's a lot of power here. I've felt power like this only on some Native American reservations. These places are needed now. It's important that you realize what you've got here—and use it."

Aysha offered to do an exorcism and next day, at dusk, we went down into the creep, the fogou's narrow side chamber. She told me to close my eyes and remain silent, noting whatever images came. She sat near me doing her breathing.

After a while I imagined I could see hooded figures in a circle crouching over something. Then flames seemed to leap out of the circle's centre and the figures retreated.

"That fits," said Aysha after I told her what I had seen. She looked out of the creep and sighed. "It's clear now. The energy can flow again."

She described how two hundred years earlier a Satanic cult had brought a pregnant woman to the creep and sealed her in. Immediately after giving birth, she had been slaughtered and the baby taken for the cult's purposes. The evil had remained and this was the source of the curse.

Aysha advised Angela and me to leave the place for ten days, because as a result of the exorcism a lot of energy would be released. By some design of fate we were due to go to Brittany for two weeks holiday the very next day.

Three days later we were at Carnac — the site of the world's biggest concentration of megaliths. There, in the Museum of Prehistory, I found a carving which precisely corresponded with Freda's description of Clwydd.

The fogou stayed with me, haunted me, pressed me to learn about it. There were the facts in the library, and then there were my own feelings and images that arose spontaneously whenever I sat with the fogou. If I was to be the new guardian, then something was required of me. I did not know what that was, but the least I could do was to find out more about its history and the people who had been here before. One way or the other, I had to write about it. It was as if the fogou wanted to speak, and it needed a voice.

6

Devil's work

Hum and thrum, run and drum
Call the Nameless One to come.
Dance around, shake the ground,
Raise his spirit with our sound.
Water and Earth to give him birth.
Air and Fire to raise him higher.
Hum and thrum, run and drum ...

Within the protective circle of the old stone walls ten naked figures danced in the moonlight around a blazing fire. Smoke rose in spirals from the crackling brushwood wreathing upraised arms and stamping feet. Round and round they danced, calling and shouting, shaking and stamping, summoning forces, conjuring a vortex that sucked in power.

A swirl of ether was forming in the centre of the circle. But the dancers, now approaching a frenzy, scarcely seemed to notice. They were oblivious, also, to three cowled figures who appeared at the edge of the circle.

Two men were supporting a woman who was half slumped between them. Every now and then her legs buckled and the men had to stop her from falling.

With a final cry the dancers fell to the ground. All except one — a woman, who remained standing, arms outstretched, gazing upwards. She gestured with a hand and a chalice was thrust into it. She raised the chalice above her, then brought it slowly down to rest against her belly, where she rolled it from side to side, muttering incantations. Then, holding the chalice in front of her, she approached the teetering woman, and nodded to the two men, who removed her cowl and forced the woman to drink.

The woman convulsed, then slowly stood upright. Hands drew her into the centre of the circle, spun her around, and positioned her legs slightly bent and apart. A bowl was brought, and an oily liquid smeared down the front of her body and rubbed slowly and deliberately between her thighs.

Then, as if out of a fog, a figure appeared in front of her, sitting cross-legged on the ground, a man's body covered in hair, eyes glazed, panting and primed with lust.

Hands edged the woman forward, her legs astride, nearly touching the upturned face. A long tongue flickered and she trembled as she was pressed downwards, arms still raised in supplication. Cloven hooves grated up her body. Her hips, poised above his, were manoeuvred for a moment, and then sank onto him.

The contractions were coming quickly now.

She lay in the dark, unable to see her attendants yet knowing they were there. Everything was black, the cloth she lay on was black, black her robe, black the symbols marked earlier on her belly. Black, too, her thoughts of the child she was soon to bear, spawned in ceremonial rut. What would it be, this babe she carried, surely not so different from any other child?

But when it came the pain was red and searing as though she would be torn in two. So sharp the pain, she feared lest perhaps the baby might have horns.

"It comes. I feel it." Dark voices, solemn.

Hands groped.

"Oh no!"

"Oh yes. Now you must work, my girl."

"It's tearing me, my God."

"Hush, don't speak that name."

"Forgive me. Oh my Lord."

"She raves. Quick, the knife and be done."

She heard a scuffle then felt the knick of sharp steel. Her cries hit the underground granite passage and ran down the walls in streams.

She cried for the sacred blood of Christ to wash her clean, to purify her for her sin, to purge her of the beast that had penetrated her womb with its foul seed. She cried for mercy by the grace of her mother's soul, cried for deliverance, swore allegiance, pleaded redemption.

And then no more pain. In its place a slippery warm living thing between her legs.

"'Tis a male."

"Let me see."

"No. No light for this child."

"Let me hold him. He's mine."

"He's not yours and never was."

"I want him."

"Be still."

"Give him back to me!"

Hands pushed her roughly back to the ground, then there was more scuffling and a grating sound. She crawled forwards slowly, weakly, reaching in front with one hand to feel her way, and then collapsed as her belly began to contract again, inches from the boulder that sealed her in.

Later, she lay in the slime of her afterbirth, clawing at the rock, straining to hear the sounds which carried through the cracks in the granite walls. She sobbed and moaned in response to the incantations and chorused intonations. And then the sounds climaxed in a shriek and she knew the Devil's work was done. Her fingernails grated downwards, tearing on the stone.

The boulder was moved back. She saw hooded figures in the flickering torch light and the flash of a curving blade. She made to dash forwards, but recoiled as a flaming brand was thrust at her face. The figures advanced. Scrabbling back she bumped against the far wall of the fogou and, with no escape, huddled whimpering.

Cowled faceless shapes loomed around her. The sword was raised. She hugged her knees, screwed her eyes shut, and began to pray.

7

The Haunt of Owls

The passage filled with rotting leaves from season after season of death and rebirth. A rich humus now covered the stone floor moistened by the rains which filtered through the cracks in the granite roof. Outwardly there was peace. But in another reality the energies were startled and scattered.

For years the fogou and the Grambler Grove remained a secret, dreaded place where people feared to go. For some, like the witches, this was used to advantage.

One night in March 1646, near the end of the Civil War, a party of Royalists, fleeing the advancing Parliamentary troops led by Fairfax, became separated from the Prince of Wales, who was escaping to the Isles of Scilly. Exhausted, hungry and lost, they stumbled through the woods near the Grambler Grove towards the lights of the mansion where they had been told there might be safety.

The last of the Levellis, a staunch Royalist, led them back through the undergrowth to the fogou where he concealed and fed them for several days. Two air vents — now plugged — which may have been made by those presumably terrified men can still be seen in the fogou's roof.

During the next century the fogou became a refuge for smugglers, and the spoils of the "wreckers" in the nearby Lamorna Cove.

Trading ships laden with wines and spirits were lured onto the rocks by lights simulating warning beacons. The "wreckers" would plunge into the boiling surf braving impalement by flying spars to grab what casks remained intact before the "Preventive", or coastguard, arrived. Crosbie Garstin, author of *The Owls' House*, who lived and wrote here in the 1920s, describes what must have been a typical scene:

> The pack train was spread out for a quarter of a mile up the valley. ... In case of a raid by mounted men who could pursue, it would be folly to go on to St Just. They were to hide their goods at some pre-ordained spot, hasten home, and lie doggo.
>
> The pre-ordained spot was the "Fogou", an ancient British dwelling hidden in a tangle of bracken a mile to the north-west, a subterranean passage roofed with massive slabs of granite, lined with moss and dripping with damp, the haunt of badgers, foxes and bats. By midnight, Eli had his cargo stowed away in that dark receptacle thoughtfully provided by the rude architects of the Stone Age, and by one o'clock he was at home in bed, prepared to prove he had never left it.[8]

It was during this time that a lintel closing the far end of the fogou was levered up and rolled away. Barrels could now be dumped inside speedily and the hole concealed, and two exits made for a quick getaway. The dank chamber witnessed drunken nights, bodies propped against walls lined with oaken casks.

Its natural inhabitants, spirits of a more ethereal kind, retreated into the crevices.

Later in the eighteenth century, the site attracted attention from visiting parties of antiquarians who came from nation-wide to ponder on the enigmatic nature of the place:

> At a few hundred yards distance from the Pipers, we came on what was considered of greater interest than anything else visited in the day. This was the Fogou (Cornish, "a cave"), a subterranean gallery with two smaller chambers. The principal passage is about thirty-

six feet in length and six feet high. Near the entrance is an opening which leads to another chamber about thirteen feet in length and four feet high. An opening has been made in the extremity of the main chamber. Through this nearly all the company passed. Learned archaeologists descended to the proper entrance, were then lost to view for a few moments, and finally reappeared at the opposite end, with different opinions as to the object of this peculiar structure. ... At the evening meeting Lord Dunraven said he had seen a great number of caves of this kind, and that it was very singular that forts nearly always possessed them. He had that day seen the remains of a fort around the cave the moment he looked for them.[9]

In 1910 the fort was finally obliterated. The quarry at Lamorna Cove, from which granite was used to build part of the Thames Embankment, provided the stone for a large house where the Iron Age huts had once stood. The granite blocks were cut by hand and then carted by horse a mile up Lamorna Lane to the site. The fort's palisades were knocked down and the stones incorporated into a garden wall, the whole area landscaped and beautified.

The house, called Rosemerryn — which means "brambly heath" — was built by an artist, Benjamin Leader. Many artists had moved to the area which had become fashionable with the success of the "Newlyn School". On adjoining land a house and studio had a short time previously been built by an associate of Stanhope Forbes, the founder of the school.

Benjamin Leader was the eldest son of Benjamin Leader Williams, who was a close friend of Constable and one of the most successful landscape painters of his day.[10] The younger Benjamin had an eye for architecture and he built the house in the style of a Cornish manor with low-beamed ceilings and pitch-pine timbers. The grounds were a blaze of rhododendrons, azaleas and camellias tended by two full-time gardeners. An area was levelled for a grass tennis court, which provided amusement for the local gentry on hot summer afternoons. But he did not live long to enjoy it. In 1916, in the Great War, he was killed in action.

In 1928 Rosemerryn was bought by a writer — Crosbie Garstin — who had just found success with the publication of *The Owls' House, High Noon* and *The West Wind*, (all recently republished). Forty years old, he had lived a life of adventure, working in lumber camps in Canada, as a miner on the Pacific coast, a ranger in Africa, and as an army horse-master and intelligence officer. A private man, he may well have found Rosemerryn provided the sanctuary he needed from a frivolous age.

His three novels recount the adventures of the "Penhales", whose home "Bosula", the Owls' House, is more than likely located where Rosemerryn now stands.

Garstin knew of Rosemerryn before he owned it. He lived and wrote next door for a while. In his novels he changed some of the names in the landscape and told only one person, his wife Lillian, where "Bosula" actually was.[11] In any event, his description of the the Owls' House precisely fits Rosemerryn:

> Bosula — "The Owls' House" — lay in the Keigwin Valley about six miles south-west of Penzance. The valley drained the peninsula's bare backbone of tors, ran almost due south until within a mile and a half of the sea, formed a sharp angle, ran straight again, and met the English Channel at Monks Cove. A stream threaded its entire length, its source a holy well on Bartinny Downs ... [12]
>
> Bosula stood at the apex of the angle, guarded on all sides ... In winter, looking down from the hills, you could barely see Bosula for trees; in summer not at all. They filled the valley from side to side and for half a mile above and below the house. Oak, ash, elm and sycamore, with an undergrowth of hazel and thorn. Near the house the stream narrowed to a few feet, ran between banks of boulders ... great uneven blocks of

granite, now covered with an emerald velvet of moss or furred with grey and yellow lichen. ... But it was the owls that were the feature of the spot. Winter or summer they sat on their boughs and hooted to each other across the valley, waking the woods with startling and eerie screams.[13]

In 1930 Crosbie Garstin vanished. No one knows for certain what happened to him. Some say he escaped to one of the exotic eastern lands he wrote about. It appears he drowned while rowing back to a friend's yacht after a party. The boat capsized and, although the woman he was with survived, Garstin's body was never found. Many con-sidered this mysterious since he was an excellent sailor and swimmer.

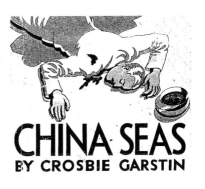

The cover of China Seas, by Garstin (Chatto & Windus, 1930)

Possibly the "Owls' House" had worked its magic on him. On the last page of his last book — *China Seas*, written at Rosemerryn in a room which overlooks a garden of rhododendrons—there is a curious premonition of his death.

> Heavily he sank beside her ... felt her arms go round him clinging desperately as to the last refuge in a yawning sea ... A bank of rhododendrons with crimson flowers ... fading fast, fading away ... [14]

It was not until 1957, when the fogou was excavated by Dr E. B. Ford, that it began to show its secrets. Ten pieces of pottery, some patterned, some with a dark glaze, were found dating from the Iron Age, La Tène B period. Removal of earth and debris from the far end of the main passage revealed that the rock had been cut away to form a shelf, possibly to serve as a shrine.

Then, while working near the entrance, Dr Ford noticed some strange markings on a boulder. He felt sure they were not accidental, and after he had studied them carefully for a while, they seemed to take the form of a figure.

He arranged for the boulder to be photographed with infrared film and the resulting photograph revealed

> a male figure, apparently full-faced, with long hair around the head, the left side of the face being flecked away. The right arm, raised from the elbow, supports a spear; the left is held horizontally to the elbow, the forearm being lifted vertically, the hand grasping a lozenge-shaped object ... possibly the head of a serpent, one of the coils of which being dimly suggested round the wrist.

Although related to similar figures in Brittany, the carving was unique in Britain.

The whole fogou site, including the fort, was attributed to the dwelling of a chieftain of the Romano-British or pre-Roman Celtic period:

> Careful consideration of the plan of the fogou and its unusual features, the two-chambered creep, the curved north end, the carved figure, suggests its use for a purpose so far unascribed to any Cornish structure of a similar type and period, namely, that of some religious usage. ... If, as is possible, the figure symbolizes a Celtic or Romano-British deity (it) might represent its presiding genius, thus establishing a unique function for the building as a temple for the religious use of the occupants of the fort.[15]

After being hidden, and sometimes abused, for two thousand years, Clwydd's place had at last been found.

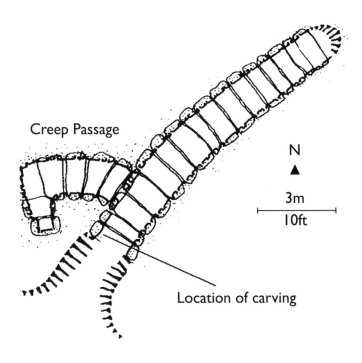

Creep Passage

N

▲

3m

10ft

Location of carving

Fogou plan (Craig Weatherhill, Belerion, Alison Hodge, 1981)

The Gypsy caravan (Claire Lucas)

8

'*My* teaching is hard ...'

While Angela and I were at Carnac, a young couple, David and Judy, came upon the fogou. A friend who lived locally thought they would like to see it. None of them knew about the exorcism that had taken place three days earlier.

As they walked toward the site, David felt he was in a dreamworld. The woods were a dazzle of colour. Pink and red rhododendrons and azaleas cascaded around them, the ground was swathed in bluebells. They climbed through the woods and reached the fogou. David, who knew nothing of earth energies and disliked underground places, felt drawn in. Judy and her friend waited outside.

As David sat against the wall in the passage, a warm feeling came over him. He felt welcome, at home. The feeling grew stronger and reached into his heart, releasing tears. He wept gently, not knowing why, and knew he would have to return.

Outside, Judy saw a figure emerge from the entrance. It was a woman dressed in white. The figure moved to the edge of Judy's field of vision and stopped. Judy was stunned. Nothing like this had ever happened to her before.

She had a sense that the fogou needed cleansing and in some way wanted to use her body as a channel. She also felt she had a choice. Something was asking her if she was willing to do this. Whatever it was had caught hold of her, but she was still free to choose. She assented.

She went into a trance state and saw, just above the fogou, a swirling purple cone. Then crows in one of the nearby pines flocked out of the branches and spiralled, flapping and squawk-ing over the fogou. She felt a rush of energy go through her body, and the cone disappeared.

Then she heard an inner voice say: "If you choose, you can give the energy back to the earth. But you must remove all blocks to your own energy. If you do not do this, it could kill you."

Shortly after we returned from Brittany, David called at the house. He had met us a month or so previously at a party, although he did not know that we owned Rosemerryn. We had mentioned casually that we were thinking of buying an old Romany caravan. Now, difficulties with his landlord were making him look for somewhere else to live. He remembered our conversation, and when he found out where we lived, knew he had to follow it up. A month later he moved to Rosemerryn and set up home in the Gypsy wagon.

Meanwhile Judy was spending a couple of months in Ireland at the Atlantis community. On her return she took digs in Penzance. She also had difficulties with her landlord, and in July she too found herself living at Rosemerryn.

"There's something I have to tell you although I don't know what it means." It was Freda on the telephone. "Just before I left Rosemerryn, I took two cuttings which I've kept in a jar by my desk. Today they fell apart. I'm also getting the message that Angela must go out into the world in some way. I'm sorry if this doesn't make much sense."

But it did make sense. Our marriage had been going through a crisis, and in October Angela and our two young children moved out. My obsessive activity and neglect of relationship had caught up with me. She had found someone else. I was devastated.

David, Judy and I decided to stay on at Rosemerryn and run it as a centre. I had already given it a name — CAER, Centre for Alternative Education and Research, *Caer* being

Celtic for "fort". We felt we had been drawn together for a purpose and the house should now be made available for others in the form of residential workshops in various aspects of personal development. I resolved to stay at Rosemerryn for as long as the centre remained viable. I guessed that after providing for my family, that might not be for very long, as I had only a minus figure to live on. However, I felt very well supported by David and Judy. They became friends and committed working partners. Each in their own way would attend to aspects of the centre that I felt less well equipped to deal with. David felt committed to building a sense of community. Judy gave her energy to the house. And all three of us felt responsible for nurturing the spirit of the place. We complemented, and learned from, each other.

Freda communicated with me many times over the next few months. She said this was a period of testing for me in which I was to get my feet firmly on the ground, that something important was required of me and that the centre would soar like a balloon. Her predictions were for the most part startlingly accurate.

I was enthusiastic about our new project but, in spite of David and Judy's support, was still crippled by the loss of my family. One evening during supper together, the pain welled up in me so acutely I had to leave the room. I stumbled to what was then the study, collapsed in a chair and began to wail.

The next thing I knew, I was looking down at myself from a corner of the ceiling. I was no longer in my body and could see myself slumped in the chair as clearly as if I had been someone else. "Jo", the chair, carpet, colours and textures were clearly defined. It was as if I had a video camera linked to my brain from a point three metres above my head, and then my essence flashed up the link. "I" was the lens.

Detached from the wailing, I knew it was necessary, and that it would pass. That, down there, was old "Jo". Here, in this calm place, was a different Jo, a new Jo. Old Jo would have to die and give way to something else. I looked down on him with great compassion.

And then I snapped back.

I looked up at the ceiling, startled. The pain had gone, I felt at peace, and also some excitement. I knew about "Out-of-the-body" experiences but never thought one would happen to me. This was an important experience because it showed me that there was another way to be, and that my pain at this time was transitory.

Some time later I experienced what I can only call a materialization.

It was early morning and I was just coming out of sleep. I was in what is called a "hypnogogic state" on the edge of sleeping and waking consciousness. I felt a pair of hands grasp the sides of my head firmly. Another hand gripped my right hand. The hands were very old, benign and female. I just knew that. Then something made passing motions in front of my face, as if to wake me up, and another arm shielded me.

I observed all this going on with interest. After all, the presences felt benign.

And then with a shock I realized that this wasn't a dream, it was actually happening. I tried to call out to the others in the house, but I could only manage a croak. The presences evaporated.

The "old ones" have never returned again, at least not in that way. My guess is that they do not want to frighten me.

David, Judy and I drew strength from a shared sense that we were part of something bigger than we understood. There had been so many synchronicities, psychic messages and even psychic phenomena. On the night of Boxing Day 1980, we decided to hold a seance using the ouija.

We crouched around the circle of letters by candlelight, our fingers resting on an upturned glass. I was sceptical. It seemed like a parlour game.

The glass moved instantly.

"Who are you?" Judy asked.

"Clwydd ... My teaching is hard. Save your children. War only short time away. Live close to life and death. You will need it."

"Does that mean it's going to be like it used to be here?"

"Always has been a hidden sanctuary."

"How do we become like you?"

"Become like yourself."

"What should we do?"

"Pay relics their just dues."

"Which relics?"

"Fogou."

"How should we use it?"

"Open it. Take down boarding. Allow it daylight."

"Why?"

"Because it must free flow."

"The creep too?"

"It should be dark. But fogou shouts."

"Overexcited?"

"Release energy. Then cover. Only when you feel right. Use power for selves. Absorb it. You need much energy to get CAER going. Close it at full moon."

"Should we work the land as you used to?"

"You cannot survive unless you do ... World must change."

"How should we use Rosemerryn? Just work the land?"

"No. You forget love. You have power. We say heal people. Hurt you, but be loving. See power. We see ourselves with you. Love-power. You can do much."

"What will help me let my love out?" I asked.

"Seek woman of spirit."

"Who?"

Names of women I knew followed.

"Be loving. Woman sees you. Go with her to the Isle of Glass. She has love. Magic woman. Go put yourself down her way."

"What should we do more of here?"

"You must find it for yourself."

I followed up the message and entered a brief relationship with the "magic woman". She helped me begin to open my heart. Fifteen years later I am still with a "woman of spirit". I have piles of notes from the fogou urging me to be strong yet open as I endured times of passion and intensity followed by separation. The physical distance between where we lived mirrored a gap within ourselves. "When will we be together?" I would ask the fogou. "When you have found yourselves," it would reply. And so "finding myself" became my path.

When I first came to live at Rosemerryn, I believed largely in what I could see. My concern had been to get the land and house into shape, to deal in practical things. But the power of the place pressed in on me, pushed me, jolted my fixed beliefs. Extraordinary events happened with remarkable speed to change me and the course of my life. A large part of me wanted to reject all notions of the "psychic" or "spiritual" or "presences". After all, even if they existed, weren't they just distractions on the path of enlightenment? Nevertheless, with something of a scientific attitude — for that had been my formal training—I decided to adopt a working hypothesis that such occurrences might be valid, and that there might be more to reality than what I perceived. I decided to remain open.

None of the events that followed persuaded me to abandon my hypothesis.

9

*E*arth force, Life force

A magical landscape surrounds the fort. It contains the densest concentration of prehistoric sites in the British Isles. This is particularly true of the parish of St Buryan in which the fort lies. Nowhere are you further than a short walk from some ancient or sacred site, a stone circle, standing stone, well, cross, ancient village, fort, beacon hill, logan stone, burial chamber or mysterious grove.

These sites conform to a pattern and the experiences that many people have had at them also seem to have a pattern. Later I shall be looking at these experiences, but first we need to understand the physical context in which they occur.

If you look beyond the roads, villages and agricultural development, you can glimpse a much older order. This is not difficult in the Land's End area because it is still relatively unspoilt. This order seems to be concerned with the shape and natural features of the landscape itself. Or, putting it another way, it shows sensitivity to the body of a living planet — Mother Earth.

Today, we build for convenience, roads are cut through hills, and fields are enlarged, to suit the needs of machines and banks. Past cultures lived in greater harmony with the earth, partly because, lacking the technology, they had to. But more than this, they saw the earth as the great provider and based their religion on it. Supernatural powers and subtle energies were all around them. Because of this, the order they imposed on the landscape harmonized with these energies and drew from them.

The fort site lies within a network of ley lines. These are lines or currents of energy which flow above and below the surface of the earth, in much the same way that acupuncture meridians convey life force, or *chi*, through the body. The ancient people of prehistory, necessarily living in close communion with nature, the seasons and the body of the earth, were sensitive to these currents and the way they ebbed and flowed. Some suggest that animals have this sensitivity and this explains their preferences for certain tracks across the countryside, and also the migratory movements of birds. It may also account for the ability of certain native peoples to navigate without modern instruments.

The planet is a living organism. Ancient peoples knew this and sited their sacred places and temples on points of the earth where this power was felt to be strongest. Many of these "power spots" are to be found at naturally occurring places of change or movement in the landscape, such as hills or wells. The Chinese science of *feng shui* is directed at locating dwellings and other buildings at places in the landscape where the flow of energy is favourable to those living there, and to readjust the flow when it isn't.

Stone circles, holy wells, beacon hills, many churches and other prominent features of our familiar landscape do not occur randomly, but are linked by an invisible interconnecting web of ley lines. Those who argue against these lines say that you can draw a line almost anywhere on a map and find a consistency about the kind of features that fall on it. Railways and petrol stations, for example, are connected in straight lines that occur statistically above chance and there is nothing mysterious about them.

But it is perhaps more helpful to look at things the other way around. Ley lines do not exist because ancient sites can be connected by straight lines on a map. Rather, the pattern or flow of the landscape suggests what is appropriate to build. The purposeful meanderings of railways and roads determine where the appropriate stops should be. In the same way, the flow of energy through the earth indicates, to those who are sensitive, which spots will be most powerful or sacred. In the end, the test is to see whether there is anything special about these places.

At least three ley lines meet at the fort site. One of these is "local" and runs for about five miles, beginning at the site of a ruined chapel on the coast at St Loy's Cove and passes through three standing stones, the Merry Maidens stone circle, a Bronze Age grave, the fogou, the site of a medieval chapel, two wells and the parish church of Penzance.

The second line could be called "national" since it runs from the abbey at Bury St Edmunds and passes through Avebury rings, Glastonbury Tor, St Michael's Brentor, the Cheesewring on Bodmin moor, and St Michael's Mount. This is the Michael Line, so named because it passes through several churches and other sites dedicated to St Michael. Extended westwards beyond St Michael's Mount it passes right by the fort. John Michell calls this a "dragon line".[16] (St Levan church, which lies near the end of the line, has an old oak rood screen emblazoned with Celtic dragons.) The third ley line which passes through the site may be part of a much larger system coming from the continent. It seems that there is a major flow of terrestrial energy connecting the Land's End with Brittany which meets the British Isles somewhere off Mount's Bay and then curls off in three directions. One branch goes up the Michael Line, a second heads off to the Isles of Scilly, and the third goes straight up the Lamorna valley across the peninsula.

This idea comes from Peter Dawkins, who, with Sir George Trevelyan, visited the fogou in the early 1980s with a party from the Gatekeeper Trust. Although it is virtually impossible to verify, there are certain physical links between Brittany and West Penwith that are consistent with the idea. Mont St-Michel in Brittany is oriented towards St Michael's Mount in Cornwall on a bearing of 300 degrees. This is the bearing of a major alignment at Carnac, the massive concentration of sacred sites in southern Brittany. The Lamorna ley is itself oriented directly towards Brittany. Rock formations and strata below the surface of the earth, as indicated on geological maps, seem to echo this energetic flow.

This ley line connects the mouth of Lamorna Cove, the fogou, a Celtic cross at a well-known haunted site, a major stone circle — Boscawen-Un, Bartinney Hill and castle (the highest in Penwith), the parish church of St Just, and Kenidjack Castle—a promontory hill fort on the north coast.

The area around the Lamorna ley line has a natural symmetry which Peter Dawkins calls a landscape temple.[17] A landscape temple is an area that has a unity and harmony in its physical features which ancient occupants venerated and

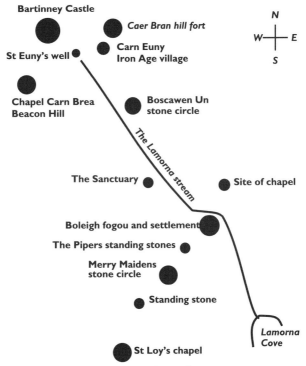

The Lamorna landscape temple (OS Land's End)

imbued with sanctity. The Lamorna "temple" has at its head three hills — the tallest being Bartinney, which is flanked on either side by Chapel Carn Brea (the first, or last, beacon hill in the land) and Caer Bran (an Iron Age hill fort). At the base of Bartinney are the twin holy wells of St Euny (notable for their legendary healing powers) from which rises a sacred stream which courses down to Lamorna Cove.

The ley runs straight up the valley containing this stream. Near the twin wells lie the remains of the Iron Age village of Carn Euny, which also has a well-preserved fogou. Carn Euny has many features similar to the better-known ancient village of Chysaucester nearby, which is generally accepted as having been a kind of "university" or Druidic place of knowledge, given the layout and construction of its "courtyard houses". Carn Euny, too, may have had a similar function as a seat of Druid learning and guardianship of the landscape temple.

Not far from Carn Euny is Boscawen-Un stone circle, the central circle in a network of Bronze Age temples at the Land's End, and, as late as the Dark Ages, the site of one of the three Gorsedds — or meeting places of the Bards — in the British Isles. This may have been the centre of the most important megalithic complex southwest of Stonehenge.

Further down the valley, wherever a road crosses the "sacred stream" there is a Celtic Cross. Just south of St Buryan church, which was built on the site of another circle, a few square miles bordering the stream appear to be "fenced off" by no less than six Celtic crosses. In the middle of this area and not far from the stream are the remains of a site known as the Sanctuary, a small group of buildings surrounding a holy well which were still occupied by Celtic monks when the Saxons invaded. Legend has it that before Athelstan, the Saxon leader, crossed over to the Isles of Scilly to complete his occupation of Cornwall, he visited the monks, stayed the night as their guest, and, as a result of a dream, promised them that if his expedition was successful he would grant them special privileges. On his return he declared the area to have the right of sanctuary, where anyone could stay unmolested. One can only guess that Athelstan sensed something about the area that made it worthy of protection.

Today, the site is little more than a couple of ruined walls in the bank of a hedge at the bottom of a muddy field. But you may still see the remains of a garden of fruit trees tended by an old farmworker who was drawn mysteriously to the spot up till twenty years ago. Ruined and forgotten, it exudes a feeling of peace and power.

From the Sanctuary traces of a path lead to the Merry Maidens stone circle, centre of another megalithic complex originally containing two other circles and many other outlying stones. This site's name comes from the Cornish *daunce maen* meaning "dancing maidens", which may be a corruption of *zanz meyn* — "sacred stones". The layout of the circle and surrounding stones suggest a *via sacra* or sacred processional route.

Several people have had strange experiences at the Merry Maidens, perhaps the best known being Tom Lethbridge's account of a stone rocking wildly while he was dowsing it.[18] The farmer who owns the land told me that during the last war a team of shire horses was hitched to the largest stone to pull the circle down so that the field would be easier to plough. Local feelings that this was a bad move were confirmed when the lead horse dropped dead.

The circle was probably originally used by priestesses for ceremonies based on lunar cycles. Its nineteen stones—a lunar number—form two crescents of nine stones, the waxing and waning moon, pincering a king — or solar — stone. Every nineteen years a calendar based on the moon's movement coincides with our solar calendar—they both have the same number of days. One of the oldest paintings in Europe depicting some form of religious ceremony apparently shows nine women, representing the New Moon (Virgin), the Old Moon (Crone), and Full Moon (Mother), advancing in a crescent to devour a young male—the "king" or "sun".[19]

The Merry Maidens (John Clark)

The processional route passes through the centre of the circle by the "king stone" and out again between the two crescents. Continuing eastwards a few hundred yards it aligns with Borah, "the place of the witch".

At one time this whole area, more densely populated than it is now, was witness to intense spiritual activity. Almost certainly this owed something to the nature of the landscape itself. Ancient people knew that there were powerful energies here and they worked with them in their own ways and for their own reasons. When Christianity came, these ways were forgotten or went underground. People feared the witch, sometimes rightly when her art, for selfish ends, was black, but often wrongly through ignorance of a much older religion.

Whatever form this activity took it was close to the body of Mother Earth. Their temples were not sited by accident. They form a pattern; they relate to the heavenly bodies; they incorporate features of the landscape.

The Lamorna temple is like a microcosm of the human body with energy centres in the landscape corresponding to chakras in the human body. The three hills of Bartinney, Caer Bran and Carn Brea are said to be the spiritual centres of the temple, where the energy in the land is at its most refined and vibrating at the highest frequency, the realm of higher beings and angelic forms. Boscawen-Un circle is the heart centre of the system, radiating energy to the wider landscape. And the fortified settlement at Rosemerryn is the sacral centre, the seat of the will, the energy here vibrating at a lower rate, manifesting itself as devas and nature spirits and other energetic forms more easily detected by human senses.

This energy is immediately "felt". Casual visitors may simply sense a special atmosphere, but to live here and become more familiar with it is to experience how the energy in the land interacts with our own energy, fuelling it or depleting it depending on what sort of state we are in. It shows in changes of mood, in the way we react to situations, in variations in our sensitivity and also in the kinds of things we become sensitive to. If the pattern of our lives is to hold down energy and suppress feelings because we are afraid of them, then the energy here will accentuate this. We are then forced either to become aware of what we are doing and be different, or else to escape because we can't stand it. And this is an act of will.

The possibility of an "energy effect" is borne out by a similarity between the fogou and Wilhelm Reich's "orgone accumulator". Reich spent the later part of his life researching "orgone", or life energy. He was Freud's favourite student for a while until they disagreed about fundamental principles of psychology. Dr Reich's experiences in treating patients led him to discover that life energy and the way in which we prevent it from flowing through our bodies was at the root of psychological disorder. Although considered a crank during his time, his work has had an impact on psychotherapeutic techniques in recent years. Towards the end of his life he built an apparatus for accumulating energy — the orgone accumulator — which he used for restoring vitality to, and healing, his patients.[20] I met his daughter, Eva Reich, at a workshop in London. She is a medical practitioner and she told me that she still uses small accumulators with her patients to assist the healing of wounds.

Orgone accumulators are constructed of alternate layers of organic and inorganic material. Organic matter attracts energy from outside and inorganic matter reflects it back inside. The accumulator works by sucking in and holding energy. A powerful accumulator would have several alternating layers, although one layer is sufficient for it to work.

The fogou is constructed in a similar manner. It was built by cutting a deep trench, lining it with (inorganic) granite and covering the whole thing with (organic) soil.

A well-recorded property of an orgone accumulator is the effect it has on body temperature. After being in one for a few minutes, body temperature rises even when the air temperature is kept constant inside and outside the accumulator.

A similar effect occurs inside the fogou. This has nothing to do with the air temperature but can actually be measured with a clinical thermometer. Body temperature rises between 0.2 and 0.4 of a degree after a few minutes. This effect is consistent and repeatable.

Another curious physical phenomenon which indicates an accumulation of energy is the "Geiger-counter effect".

The fogou was the subject of a survey for the Dragon Project, an enquiry conducted by associates of *The Ley Hunter* to provide scientific evidence for the possible original purpose of stone circles and other ancient sites. One anomaly they discovered was high-frequency sound vibrations emanating from stone sites, which varied with sunrise and sunset. The second kind of variation they recorded was radioactivity.

Choosing West Penwith because of its high density of granite, which naturally has a high level of radioactivity, they compared Geiger-counter readings at several stone circles and also in the fogou. They found that the level of radioactivity inside the stone circles was half that outside. The circles seem to create a protected space. By remarkable contrast, the reading inside the fogou as compared with the outside was double. The fogou seems to act as an accumulator.[21]

The fogou is an energetically powerful place which is

worthy of respect. Its dark and silence can assist you to go inside yourself and listen to an inner voice, see with your inner eye, or feel the heightened sensations of energy in the body. It still has healing powers and can give guidance to those who seek it—as we shall see.

10

Initiation and Healing

The fogou's carving depicts a Celtic god of healing. Similar figures are to be found in Brittany and elsewhere. One suggestion is that this is Clew an Nemed, which means "Clew of the Sanctuary", although there are other possibilities. Since it is equally weathered on either side, and not just on the side exposed to the fogou's entrance, it was most likely brought from another site, possibly a Druidic grove or sanctuary, and would therefore predate the building of the fogou.[22]

The fogou's snake, unique in Britain, may owe something to its proximity to the St Michael "dragon". I have even heard, from a local visitor, that there are legends which tell of a dragon living in the fogou.

Both the snake, or serpent, and the dragon are traditionally symbols for the flow of life force or energy. In Tantric and Yogic disciplines the path to enlightenment coincides with the awakening of energy which resides at the base of the spine and which rises up the chakras as they open. Kundalini Yoga

The fogou's carving (computer enhanced, Jo May)

describes two channels twining either side of the spine, *ida* and *pingala*, corresponding to the masculine and feminine principles. Kundalini energy is depicted as a serpent. The ancient Chinese saw dragons in the landscape which for them represented the flow of terrestrial energy. The massive serpentine landscape temple at Avebury was the site of seasonal invocations to fertility and the life force. The life-giving physician has as a symbol the caduceus, two snakes coiling up a staff. The Aztecs, ancient Egyptians and Druids all revered the snake as a symbol of life-giving power.

The carving may be modelled on Serapis, a god prevalent around 300BC in Roman and Greek lands who was associated with the Unconscious, Judgement, raised Kundalini, Healing and Channelling. The Celtic version of this deity was Cernunnos, and in Ireland he was known as Cerna. There are also similarities to Asclepius, a Greek god of healing, who grasps a snake in one hand and a staff in the other. Cernunnos also holds a snake, but in his other hand he is shown holding a torc. Cernunnos was a guardian of the underworld.[23]

The theme is of Kundalini energy, serpent power, raised and mastered. Raised energy brings up unconscious material which must be faced and integrated. The god of healing is a guardian of the underworld into which the initiate must enter in order to confront his or her unconscious. It takes a hero to encounter the dragon in its lair, free the damsel and find the treasure hoard. We enter the depths to face our personal demons, monsters and dragons. When we have confronted them, we can be free of fear and more

Interpretation of carving (from CAER's logo)

connected, because we are no longer their prisoner. This is the treasure. So entering the underworld of the unconscious is the key to healing, and this also seems to be a key to the purpose of the fogou.

It is not easy to see the carving of the God of Healing. It is best viewed from well within the passage so that the light from outside throws it into relief. It becomes visible by attending to its shadows—which, ironically, is also true of the unconscious.

Peter Dawkins gave me an account, from his own perspective, of how the fogou might have been used for initiation into healing. I think it is worth reproducing in full:

> Part of the initiatory experience is the descent into the darkest, deepest recesses of the body nature, into Mother Earth, to experience that side of man's nature to an extreme.
>
> The experience can be quite fearful at first, as a numbness, a cold almost freezing darkness and immense weight seems to press upon one, and a sense of intense aloneness in a "grave" of who knows what hidden terrors. But the initiate learns, at the most intense moment, to just love the surroundings and the condition in which he finds himself, as with an effort of will he realizes that he, as a spirit, is immortal and is born to love ...
>
> So in the depths of the grave he radiates out the Christ love, and this spiritual light melts the dense matter, illuminates the darkness and releases the energy of the dense matter. This earth energy is the Dragon, the Kundalini. And so the initiate is in effect confronting the Dragon as a St George, and piercing it with his spear of love-light. ... These earth energies are released from the darkest, densest recesses of the initiate's own being, and also from his surroundings, and they flow through his soular form ... bringing him ever nearer

perfection. His chakras are brought to flower ... his fountain of life to increase its flow, and his consciousness and abilities to unfold a thousandfold.

For the initiate who undergoes this experience while still retaining his physical body, he emerges from the tomb as one reborn, and as a person greatly enhanced in his wisdom and power to guide and lead the people on earth.

For those departing from the physical body, they are helped to transmute as much of their lower selves as is possible at that critical moment of death, lasting about three days, so that they may go on to the higher realms with as much goodness and lasting qualities as possible, that will not be lost in the fires of purgatory, and hence to find an immortality of soul.

The fogou is filled with the aura of the great love that was released here in the past, and it still retains its abilities to entomb a person in the intense stillness and weight of earth forces. ... It is a place of great sanctity, and enhanced by its siting in the chakra of a powerful landscape temple.

It is more than likely that the initiate would have entered the passage by one entrance and left via a different exit. ... There may have been more than one chamber leading off the passage, but my present feeling is that even if this was so at Rosemerryn, nevertheless only one chamber was actually necessary for the initiation. It may be that numbers undergoing initiation required more chambers. The passage part, I think, was used for preparation and teaching, while the chamber was the tomb proper, which was sealed during the three days of initiation.

The siting of the emblem, carved into a shield-shaped rock at the entrance/exit of the fogou, is a sure sign of the purpose of the structure. This to my mind was the exit (if there were two ways in and out of the fogou), and the attained initiate would be reborn into the light of day, standing at the gateway of the fogou with his right hand on the shield with its emblem of what he had attained, steadying himself, and with his left hand shielding his eyes from the light of the sun.

The stone sealing the door to the tomb would have previously been rolled away by those attending and supervising the initiatory experience, allowing the warmth and light of the dawn to creep into the chamber and awake the sleeping initiate, calling him back to life.

If it was the body of a dead person, then the bier with the body upon it, bedecked with flowers and herbs, would be carried to the fogou exit, to be bathed in the rays of the dawn star, while the released soul would be gently raised by the Master of Light in the heart of the spiritual Sun.

This stone is a typical "paladium" or shield. It is a kind of altar stone, but imbued with the properties of light and vibration that protect a holy place. Etherically they blaze with light, as if polished and reflecting the sun's rays, and this one is no exception. Its shape is an important factor in its function, which is based on the heart shape. The etheric form or energy field of it is a perfect heart form, pulsing with light. The emblem emblazoned on it thus becomes the heraldic device, spiritually, of the initiated one ...

It portrays the initiate who has pierced the dragon-serpent of the Kundalini with his or her spear of love-light, as a St George, the knight-hero, and raised the dragon-serpent up that shaft of light to become a living fountain of life and light.

This achievement is portrayed by the bearing of the spear in the right, active, masculine hand ... and by grasping in the left hand, firmly, the serpent of earth energies which have been raised up the spear (here signified by the left arm) like the symbol in the caduceus. The initiate holds the serpent in the left hand, as this is the hand or arm that is feminine, receptive, and relates therefore to the feminine serpent or soul nature (which has to be evolved, raised, from an inert ignorant state to a fully alert, erect, illumined state.) ... This is the initiation that can be undertaken in this fogou, helped by the very structure of the fogou and its ability to concentrate the earth forces and thus the experience.

One word about Arthur. Arthur dies in the final battle or initiation, and sleeps still. He cannot achieve the final initiation portrayed here until he can redeem through pure love and surrender the deeply rooted "sin" that lies in the darkest recesses of his subconscious. He has to face that weakness and strengthen it in pure love, forgiving himself and the fault, and making amends.

In such an initiation one is confronted by the darkest places of oneself. It is not an experience for the unprepared or weak-hearted. But if the soul succeeds in this "battle", although dying to his old sinful self, he will become reborn or re-awakened as a Son of the Sun, portrayed by the emblem.

It is highly significant that such a place of initiation is to be found at Rosemerryn, Lamorna, if this is also the sacral centre of the landscape temple in this area of Land's End; for the sin of the sacral centre (i.e. the unbalanced use of the energies of the sacral centre, and abuse of them) is the sin of humanity en masse, and is what we must all redeem before we truly see the Golden Age.[24]

The carving points to a time when there was concern to maintain the forces of heaven and earth in balance. The spear is held in the right hand — the side of reason, focus and the masculine, and the snake is held in the left — the side of emotion, receptivity and the feminine. These are partly modern associations derived from research into the function of the two sides of the brain. But they also occur world-wide in other cultures with no scientific traditions. So it seems, as Peter Dawkins suggests, that those who made the carving knew about the life force and had ways of working with it for purposes of spiritual unfoldment.

One possibility seems to be this: the fogou is located in a place of power, linked with other places of power in a landscape that was in former times "worked" spiritually by a people who had knowledge that we have now lost and are only slowly rediscovering — knowledge that may be necessary for our further evolution. The "power" or energy of the place affects human energy fields, accentuating the flow of life force in our bodies and hence the patterns we evolve bodily, mentally, emotionally and spiritually in order to either contain or release those energies. Experience thus gets heightened.

There is a possibility too that such places are "edges between worlds", or gateways, where "other realities" are more easily perceptible. If we accept, then we change, and when we change we become more aware. We become more aware of ourselves, of others, and also of other realities, because they are there too. Nature spirits and beings from dimensions on the edge of ours become accessible—although we may not always talk about them, because most people would think we are crazy.

If this is the sacral centre in a larger landscape temple, then the fogou's snake is in its proper home. Kundalini, the serpent power, lies coiled at the base of the spine at the sacrum. It lies there in all of us waiting to rise as its path through the chakras becomes open, waiting to bring enlightenment, waiting to show us who we really are.

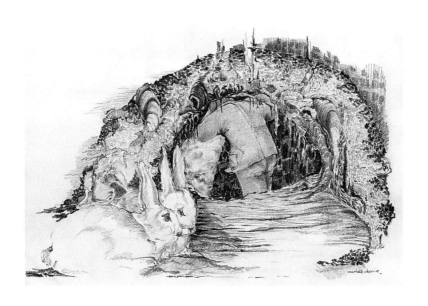

Entrance to the Underworld (Marliet Denie)

11

$\mathcal{P}$owers and Presences

Living with a fogou in the garden has convinced me that its secrets will not be discovered by bowling in, taking the odd photograph and peering at the stones. You need to be around it for a while, listen, let its presence work on you, and then it can begin to speak.

The nature of the work done at CAER has incidentally enabled a considerable amount of research on the fogou, not only by myself, but also by respected psychics, shamans from Native American and Aboriginal cultures, researchers into altered states of consciousness, and also some of the several hundred people who visit the centre each year for courses concerned with personal and spiritual development. What emerges is a pattern involving synchronous imagery, inner voices and visions, and energy effects experienced at a bodily level.

From these experiences, it seems clear that the fogou was used as a focal point for spiritual practices involving death and rebirth, vision quests, healing, inner guidance and soul-making. The reason it is located underground seems to be because it is contained in the body of the earth—the ground from which we emerge and to which we return — the Mother. In this respect it is similar to the Native American *kiva*, another underground structure for spiritual practice.

The fogou is also located directly on a line of earth energy. The current of this line appears to fluctuate with the time of day, moon's phases and the season — testable by dowsing. The fogou's location and orientation is not therefore accidental.

The legends associating the fogou with dark forms of witchcraft confirm this view. Black magic is a distortion and manipulation of white magic for selfish ends. The energy is there anyway. What makes it "good" or "bad" is how you use it. Before we were able to use the fogou for private meditation, ceremony or research, it had to be thoroughly exorcized and cleansed—a testimonial to its former abuse.

The kind of phenomena experienced in the fogou — on several occasions by a number of people simultaneously — include inner voices giving uncannily pertinent guidance, sometimes forecasting events before they happen; subjective perceptions of powers and presences — usually of female figures, frequently described as "women in white" or priestesses; visions involving fire, symbolic, perhaps, of inner cleansing; visions involving the laying-out of the dead — usually bedecked with flowers — in preparation for the soul's journey to another realm; visions of enforced entombment for the purpose of confronting the dark side of the soul in order to re-emerge reborn; experiences of people being "called" to the fogou in order to symbolically "die" or else to collectively grieve someone who actually has died; experiences of waves of peace or comfort, and stilling of inner turmoil.[25]

This chapter consists of a small sample of the range of experiences which people have reported over the years. Most of these people had little or no previous knowledge or preconceptions about the fogou. Taken as a whole, I believe they meet the criteria for "genuine impressions of another reality", which are set out in the next section.

Some of the accounts describe encounters with spirits not directly connected with the fogou. They also contain elements which have a tinge of malevolence or spookiness. All the experiences, except a couple of my own, come from published accounts or else were related to me first-hand.

In October 1981 twenty people under the guidance of John

Heron, who was then assistant director of the British Post-graduate Medical Federation, engaged in an Altered States of Consciousness (ASC) Research Group. This was a five-day residential workshop in the CAER programme which employed a method called "cooperative inquiry" for research-ing "the other reality"—a theme collectively agreed upon by the group. Several cycles of research were conducted building up to a ritual in the fogou. The results of this research were published by the Human Potential Research Project of the University of Surrey. [26] I have drawn the following from these research findings and from my own recollections of having been part of that workshop.

Each cycle of research consisted of the group as a whole initially deciding what was going to be researched and how it was going to be done. Then the group engaged in an "action phase", in which we did what we had decided to do. A "reflection phase" followed in which the group examined experiences from the "action phase", and also dealt with the possibility of collusion and delusion. The results of this cycle then fed into a next cycle, and so on.

Two of these cycles are of interest here. The first one generated criteria that can help in deciding whether percep-tions of another reality are valid or not. The second example graphically illustrates how another reality can interface with this reality. All this is relevant, since much of this book concerns itself with perceptions of another reality.

The fogou ritual, which comprised our fourth cycle of research during the workshop, was simple. We met at an agreed location in the grounds and then proceeded in a line, chanting, into the main fogou passage, where we joined hands remaining silent and open to "impressions from the other reality". We then gathered outside the fogou on top of the creep passage while a member of the group offered prayers from inside the creep. Again we were silently receptive to whatever impressions wanted to come. After this we gathered in the grouproom and shared and reflected on our experiences.

People reported: "powerful trembling and shaking" with energy surging through the body (six people); "mental and physical cleansing" (three); "impulses to act or move in various ways" (eight); a sense of two other presences in the other reality in the fogou (two); "a lot going on in the other reality" (two); strong images including faces in the walls of the main passage (five); "power" which left people feeling "in awe" and "positively shaken" (many); and phrases like "overwhelmed", "wonderful", "very good feeling", and "like a cool dip" (five).

Outside the fogou four people sensed or "saw" energy swirling out of the creep, like flames.

Summarizing, John Heron identified five different kinds of experience:

- Streaming of energy in and out of the energy field of the physical body.
- "Vision", pictures or images — of faces, symbolic objects.
- A felt sense of presences and their activities, and of subtle energies, in the other reality.
- A sense of the numinous, of pervasive spiritual power.
- Emotional uplift.

During the reflection phase the group members became concerned about the implicit assumption that we had been interacting with another reality at all. We decided to hold open the possibility that we were colluding with each other in order to delude ourselves and were confusing our "hysterically activated subjective fantasies with genuine impressions of the other reality".

On the next day we therefore devised a "systematic falsification" or "Devil's Advocate" procedure to find "quite ordinary alternative interpretations, reducing assumed Altered States of Consciousness to somewhat pathological Ordinary States of Consciousness."

The Devil's Advocate procedure involved each person

sitting in a "hot seat" and being challenged by other members of the group about statements they had made about their experiences in the fogou on the previous day. These statements had previously been recorded in writing. This is a brief sample:

> *Devil's Advocate:* Your so-called ASC impressions are nothing but a form of attention-getting through promulgation of the bizarre.
> *Reply:* This is possible; but other attention-seeking activities are less strenuous and less likely to be rejected.

> *Devil's Advocate:* Your so-called ASC impressions are a fantasy projection of your longing for the non-existent mystical.
> *Reply:* I accept that some part of my experience may be just a projection of my longing; but equally such longing may exist precisely because of the reality of what is longed for.

> *Devil's Advocate:* Your so-called ASC impressions are nothing but unexplored aspects of your psyche projected out and sucked into the mass delusion under which some of you people in Cornwall operate.
> *Reply:* I accept this as a possibility.

> *Devil's Advocate:* Your images of a warrior and a guardian are a displacement of your denied rage.
> *Reply:* I am in touch with my rage; I have had no such images prior to the procession; I did not identify and do not identify with the warrior trip.

> *Devil's Advocate:* Your images of swords are but a projection of your psychological armouring and rigidity together with blocked sexual energy.
> *Reply:* I am not heavily armoured, having worked on it a lot; and I am in touch with my sexual energy.

Devil's Advocate: You are not in touch with another reality, you are just unable to cope with this reality.
Reply: I do not accept your dichotomy: there is only one comprehensive reality.

Devil's Advocate: Your feeling of cleansing in the fogou is nothing to do with being psychic or having an ASC: it is entirely a physiological response to the physical conditions, as in any damp cave.
Reply: But I have been in other damp caves in which I have not experienced any kind of cleansing of this sort.

This is a tiny extract from a process that lasted a whole day. It was a valuable process because it highlighted the possibilities of mixing up "impressions of the other reality" with the "projection of purely psychological material". It also pointed to the possibility that "emotional longing for the other reality may be part of the evidence for it". It seemed, too, that explaining away the other reality is often "less plausible than the assertion of its existence".

Out of the Devil's Advocate process we evolved a set of criteria to help distinguish "genuine impressions of the other reality" from "purely subjective illusions". The criteria, which have "interlocking support for each other" were as follows:

1   *Agreement:* two or more persons have the same or similar impressions of the other reality.

2   *Heterogeneity:* the occurrence and the compatibility of very different sorts of impressions of the other reality, both serially and simultaneously, both in one person and in several.

3   *Synchronicity:* simultaneously occurring impressions of the other reality are meaningful in the same or in a similar way to two or more persons.

4   *Spontaneity:* impressions of the other reality often come unbidden; and the recipient did not want or intend to produce them in the way in which they occurred.

5   *Independence:* impressions of the other reality have a life of their own and they are not amenable to manipulation and interference, while their content may be unexpected and surprising.

6   *Spatial reference:* impressions of the other reality have reference to "locations out there" in a subtle and profoundly extensive "space" that is somehow within physical space.

"... Taking all these six criteria together and applying them to the manifold experiential data ... in the fogou, there is a *prima facie* empirical warrant for saying that there were presences active in terms of subtle energy ... within the physical space in and around the fogou during the time of our ritual activity there, and that what they were doing was potent, uplifting and energizing for many of us human beings present."

A further research cycle developed out of an incident which occurred spontaneously on the day following the fogou ritual. This incident involved something in "another reality" entering this reality with effects which were observed by several people. Putting it another way, the Universe presented us with an opportunity for testing our criteria.

We were working with some of the feelings that were coming up for people as a result of the research group. This was an agreed and necessary part of our agenda, to ensure the smooth flow of our inquiry. A group member was working on present feelings which took her into a "past-life experience". She returned from this journey with an imagined sword, which she "passed" around the group. The "sword" was ceremonially handed from person to person. As each person took it and weighed it, or saluted with it, or otherwise flourished it, the imaginary sword from the "other reality" seemed to take on more of a presence in "this reality". David's dog Rosie, a German shepherd, entered the room just as the sword was handed back to the original group member. She offered it to Rosie, blade first. Rosie, sniffing, examined a point in space where the sword tip would have been, then pulled back sharply with a snarl as if she had been pricked on the nose. Rosie's response was more than just surprise at nothing being there. She behaved as if she had been hurt and kept a wary distance.

The group was impressed with this, and decided that the sword needed to be disposed of in some appropriate way. The woman who had found it then "placed" it in a mirror on the wall. All this is documented in John Heron's report. What followed later is not documented because it happened a week later.

Immediately following the research group, we had another workshop which at one point also used the mirror. This was unusual in itself, because it was the only other time that the mirror had been used in a group. Because it was a different group, nobody knew about the sword. The group took the mirror down, propped it on the floor, and each person interacted with his or her reflection. The mirror, it seems, spontaneously smashed.

A rational explanation of the whole sword affair would go something like this: Rosie the dog was hypnotized into believing in the existence of a sword by the group's shared fantasy. The mirror smashed because someone dislodged it. There is no connection between these events. No sword was present in this, or in any other, reality. There is no "other reality", only this one.

An alternative explanation might go: The sword had a reality in some part of the woman's unconscious. A sword is an archetypal image that is part of the collective unconscious and was therefore also meaningful to the group. The combined energies of the group brought the sword to a point of embodiment below the threshold of human perception, but above the perceptual threshold of a dog. Rosie was hurt in her energy body. Partly embodied artefacts from the "other reality" are dangerous. The "other reality" summoned the next group to smash the mirror.

To get away from the house and groups and have some space for myself, I had built a "log cabin", not a real one, but a timber-frame construction faced with offcuts, so that it looked like a log cabin. My first night there I was "attacked". I could not sleep, felt sweaty, tossed and turned. And then in a half-sleep I imagined that things were attaching themselves to my back, creepy-crawlies, goblins, crabs and scorpions. Things were in the cabin, poking and pinching me, and I knew I had to get them out. I thought of ringing a friend who was knowledgeable about these matters, but as it was about two in the morning I knew I would have to do it myself.

Not sure quite what to do, I did everything I could think of. I visualized blue light, said the Lord's Prayer, visualized Celtic warriors in the four corners of the room, and finished off with an exorcism. The effect was like firing a canon, when a slap would have done. Whatever was in the cabin scrammed fast, and nothing has ever returned. I realized that it is not what you say or do in these circumstances that matters, but your intent, the exercise of your will. Unwanted energies need to feel that you mean business. Repeating ritualized incantations which carry the weight of the collective obviously helps. But I have the sense that in essence all they really do is say, "Go. I really mean it."

One Halloween my eldest daughter, Hannah, had two friends, Laura and Marianne, to stay the night in the house. Laura was unable to sleep. She saw, illuminated by the full moon shining through the half-drawn curtains, a small figure sitting on the end of Hannah's bed with its arms wrapped around the bedpost and its legs crossed.

It looked like a toy with long legs and arms, bushy black hair, gold round-framed spectacles, a little waistcoat, pointed feet and a very long pointed nose. The figure was looking at Hannah and then at Marianne, laughing silently.

Then it turned to Laura, and froze. It was as if it "knew" that it was being seen. Laura pulled the bedclothes over her head, frightened.

Later she described what she had seen to Hannah. Her description precisely fitted a toy that Hannah had had as a child and which she had found frightening, a toy which Laura knew nothing about.

A possible explanation is that a spirit, with mischievous intent, had probed Hannah's unconscious, located this feared image, and embodied it, presumably thinking it was all rather fun—until Laura spotted it.

Rob, a psychotherapist with a practice in Germany, and his wife Siggi lived at Rosemerryn for a period of eighteen months.

"Once when I was travelling back from Berlin on the train, I met a young woman who, when she heard where I lived, said, 'Aren't you afraid of the ghosts?' It turned out that she was related to one of the previous owners and had lived in the cottage for a while. She said there had been regular poltergeist activity and that it had happened so often they had had to move out. She said things would fly around in the sitting room like a whirlwind. Some of the taxi drivers who take people from Penzance think the whole area is spooky and that Rosemerryn and the fogou are the centre of it all."

When they first arrived at Rosemerryn Rob and Siggi often had restless nights. On waking up in the morning Siggi would say, "Those children make so much noise," although there were never children around. Later, when she was pregnant, Siggi often felt bothered by "ghosties and ghoulies" in the night.

"We had just been to see Jo who gave her the idea of using protective guardians. It was a bright, sunny morning and Siggi and I were walking down to the cabin, where we were staying, past the Gypsy caravan. I was walking in front of her, and I said a little prayer for someone to protect her while I was away in Berlin. Then I turned to look at her and I saw a man behind her, clear as daylight. He was enormous, huge. He had long flaming red hair and a big beard, and was dressed in bright colours, mainly blue and green. The thing that struck me was his sandals. They were flat with leather thongs going up his legs and he had a big sword at his side. He kind of sent me a message: 'Don't worry—I'll look after her.' Then I did a double-take and he was gone. I never mentioned this to anyone until about six weeks later when I told Judy. She said, 'Oh, that's Clwyd, the Celtic chieftain.' That was all I ever actually saw with my eyes. Siggi spent that weekend peacefully."

Some years, and another baby later, Siggi was in the hut with their two children and felt she was being haunted again. Peter, their son, also had a restless night and in the morning talked about "children playing around the hut in the middle of the night". Because of their previous experiences with "the children" this surprised them.

"Once while I was running a group, I was lying on my bed having a rest when I felt a presence. I didn't see anything, but I said, 'Oh, go away,' because by now I was getting used to them. I said it out loud, kind of offhand. It was a woman and she said, 'Don't be like that. I only want to give you a massage!' I didn't feel her touch me, but I felt someone massaging my aura. It was very pleasant."

In 1987 while conducting a three-day residential workshop on Native American teachings as part of the CAER programme a Métis Cherokee shaman spent some time in the fogou. He said he saw three female presences, all from a different time period. He also told me the following:

The fogou has a strong matriarchal feel although there are transitory male presences. The guardian, or Priestess, of the fogou is female. She has blond hair and green eyes. She wears a silver sheen robe and a gold amulet inscribed with a rising or setting sun and an H-shaped sigil. Her face oscillates between being old and young. The other two female presences are also guardians, but very young and of lesser status. One was standing behind the Priestess and the other in front, although at times they appear to merge into her.

This was a very unusual phenomenon and one the shaman had never seen before. He said he would have to check it out with his elders.

He also said there was another chamber in the fogou waiting to be discovered—more of which later.

Before he went, I asked him if he knew of any cere-monies for ensuring the continued prosperity of the centre. I explained that things were getting a little rough.

He looked at me seriously and said: "If the spirits want to get rid of you, do you know how they will do it? Through economics, through the finances. It's the easiest way."

He told me how to do a ceremony to create a "crystal dome of protection" to keep out any spirits that might be tinkering with the energy.

It was a powerful ceremony. I performed it at dusk, and as the night grew in I could feel the potency of unseen presences. David had asked if he could stay in the cottage with a lighted candle, to be connected to the place but not part of the ceremony. As things got underway, however, he felt compelled to leave.

In the years that immediately followed, the centre did indeed prosper.

Here is the ceremony the shaman gave me:

Materials: Crystals, sea salt (for cleansing the crystals), cayenne pepper, a mixture of garlic powder and sea salt (for protecting the crystals and dispersing unwanted energies), nylon line or thread (for hanging the crystals), an abalone shell (or container for burning sage), dried sage, feather (for wafting sage smoke—swan, turkey, goose, hawk, or eagle are all good).

Procedure for creating a Crystal Dome of Protection:

1   Clean and purify the crystals. This is best done by placing them in a bowl of water in which you have dissolved sea salt. Leave the bowl to stand for four days—preferably in sunlight.

2   Bless the crystals in whatever way is appropriate for you. Ask them to do what you'd like them to do — (e.g. give protection).

3   Place the crystals, preferably at dusk, as follows:

(a) One crystal (or cluster) should be placed in the main working space, or room, at each of the cardinal points (north, east, south and west). Crystals should also be placed in the outer perimeter of your space in the non-cardinal points (northeast, northwest, southeast and southwest.) These crystals can be suspended if that's more convenient.

(b) One crystal (or cluster) should be placed at each of the non-cardinal points just inside the perimeter of your whole property. These crystals can be buried. Sprinkle the mixture of cayenne, garlic and sea salt onto, and in circles around, the perimeter crystals. This will repel any forces that want to interfere with them.

As you place all the crystals, do a "banishing". (This may sound a little heavy, but it shows you mean business.) The following was given to me and works:

> I banish from this place any and all energies, vibrations, entities, spirits, forms, and manifestations that are not in absolute harmony, alignment, balance and resonance with the will of my Higher Self (or the Spirit of God, etc.). And I banish you to all eight directions. I bear you no ill will or harm. I send you with love.

You could probably use any words that felt right. It is the

intention that matters. "Listen, you guys, scram—I really mean it … " might be less effective.

A word of caution. Doing this is powerful and can stir things up — at least for the duration of the ceremony. It is advisable to perform this ceremony on your own with the house empty.

Smudging:

Sage smoke cleans up energy. It is particularly important to do this if your space contains any kind of "bad atmosphere", for example after an argument, or after any kind of emotional or therapeutic work, if that is what you do. Discharged energy can build up and provides a wonderful playpen for dark forces. It's useful to regard smudging as psychic vacuum-cleaning. It is also wise to smudge yourself and the crystals before doing the Crystal Dome ceremony.

The procedure is to put some sage in the shell, light it (a gas lighter works best), fan it with the feather, and waft the smoke around the room, not forgetting corners.

May your space shine with Beauty, Harmony and Prosperity!

The following is a selection of personal accounts that have been published elsewhere.

> One person I know simply cannot go down into Boleigh fogou — she finds the power there too over-whelming, while another just wants to curl up and sleep down there. Sometimes the fogou itself can seem not to want you to enter: someone else had a strange experience the first time she went to Boleigh. When she got there she found the entrance was covered over by two large megalithic slabs, completely blocking the way in. Thinking this was normal, she returned, only to be told later by someone that of course there was no barrier to the entrance. When she went back again, there were no entrance stones, but she swears to this day that they were there when she first saw it, and

were much too huge for anyone to have casually put there and taken away later.

Sometimes the energy or power in the fogou seems active or even malignant (or is it simply the way individual people respond to it?). One person had a ring she was wearing literally wrenched off her hand while she was down there in a way she has never been able to explain. Others, such as myself, have always found the atmosphere very peaceful, almost soporific.

—*Cheryl Straffon*[27]

[The fogou] has become a gateway to the underworld for me; it helps me reach within myself levels of dream and vision which enrich and add meaning to my life and my pictures (I am an artist.) That is not to say that the transition is always easy. The fogou has at times had odd physical effects on me — cramping stomach pains, once I was overtaken by acute dizziness, often it seems dark and unwelcoming. It is different on different occasions, or perhaps it is I who am different and at times not ready to experience its depth on my own. Going into a fogou, I meet myself.

My most intense experience in the fogou was a visual one. I had been staying at Rosemerryn to do a five-day group and about halfway through, in that fragmented depressive mood which I have always found occurs for me at this stage in a successful group, I felt the need to separate myself off from my companions and drawn towards the fogou as if the fogou contained some healing secret for me. Although apprehensive, I felt prepared to go through with this. I spent some time within the fogou that night — how long I couldn't say. I remember the feel of the mud floor against my bare feet and of the rug in which I had cloaked myself.

As I stood there in the dark, I began to feel strangely without identity or time: I was any woman in any age, looking for spiritual comfort in the fogou. It came in the form of a vision. Suddenly it was no longer dark but I appeared to be standing in daylight a little way from a church and watching a wedding party coming out of a church. The bride, groom and guests were there although I could not see faces clearly. It was a bit like watching a video in the clarity of the picture. Then I remember being distracted and feeling cold, and the vision disappeared and I went out.

This was a bizarre experience — you could say I must have dozed off and dreamt it. But, for me, the clarity and lucidity of the images made it different from a dream. In any case I was vertical the whole time and I remember thinking to myself, "Well, how odd this is!" Also over the next few days I began to see that the experience had been relevant for me on two levels: I felt more at peace with myself as the "wedding" had symbolized an inner process of male-female harmonization which had happened for me; for me it was also confirmation that it was all right for me to remarry, which I did next year, although not in a church.

—*K. G.*[28]

... An astrological weekend. What a magical setting! Lush autumnal vegetation swamped my senses, the aroma of decaying wood, of sodden grass, greens, golds and browns of September's garb ... the sweetness of bulging purple blackberries — the fullness, the ripeness of Mother Earth ... In this atmosphere I came to exchange new ideas and insights. ... Sunday morning I awoke early and roamed the grounds. Damp cloying mist enveloped my clothes, hair and eyelids; spiders' webs glistened with droplets of dew; no birdsong, an eerie silence. I returned to the kitchen for a hearty breakfast. I relate the substantial breakfast so you may realize that I was not light-headed. Our teacher then suggested that we visit the fogou in the grounds and have some time for meditation. I was puzzled to know what a fogou was: I had heard the name but knew nothing of its reputation or attendant myths or explanations for its construction and purpose.

As we reached the fogou there was still a chill in the morning air ... On entering the fogou we faintly discerned on our left the figure of the "Healing God" carved onto the rock. The dankness quickly enveloped each one of us, six women disappearing into the gloom. The passage gradually sloped downwards and after a few feet we found ourselves standing flat against the wall to avoid the large puddle. We stood quietly while four small candles pricked the darkness and gave solace. We allowed the energy from our bodies to flow down in to Mother Earth. I was feeling content and peaceful, breathing deeply as I felt the deep connection with the earth.

Then, the only way to describe the next sensation was as "a bolt from the blue". The force was immense: it was a spiralling force in the centre of my forehead, the spin was so strong, and quickly became faster and faster. I felt sick, my whole body reeling. I felt my head would explode. I could no longer stand, my knees were collapsing and I fell to the ground. As I fell, the energy left me, as suddenly as it had appeared. I was very shaken and was helped back to the kitchen ... For about an hour I lay on the floor while the workshop continued, but my concentration had gone. I felt exhausted and just wanted to curl up in a ball and go to sleep ...

From that time my life changed, an acceleration of energy and consciousness ...

—*Geraldine Andrew*[29]

A Visit to the Goddess

I didn't want to go down
to the fogou. I knew She'd be there.
I didn't have to go down
I felt tearful, not fearful
She is here, everywhere
She's not hiding
No need to seek Her out
And yet ...

A wander round the grounds
Perhaps we'll change our minds
The stream is smaller, further
away than I remember it
The trees seem further apart
Times change, perhaps it's
best to forget the past

My feet turn right,
My mind sighs no
I'm there before I no it.
A slippery slope
A leap in the dark
And suddenly I'm deep in her womb
Cool and damp with the sweet smell of earth

Be you, not them, the Goddess whispers
Your teachers are your teachers
You are different, you are special
Be yourself, dare to be you
Don't ask whose path you should follow
follow your own.
The more you, you become
The more I love you
The less I have to peer
into the darkness of your soul

to see who's there
Dare to be you. That's all. I love you.

Blasted by that awful love
I cry in my mother's womb
Swamped by emotions
I scramble away
Back to the sunlight
Inspired, refreshed, renewed

—*Eileen Herzberg*[30]

Fogou (Gabrielle Hawkes)

12

Spirits Talking

Next time you watch TV, notice how many people have their left side of the face sadder or more closed than their right. The muscles on each side of the face are controlled by the opposite side of the brain. And each side of the brain is specialized for certain functions. The right side, for example, is specialized among other things for emotions. And the right side of the brain controls the left side of the face. For so many people the emotional, creative, holistically perceiving side is shut down or asleep, and you can see this in their faces.[31]

There is an urgent need for humankind to become awake. Native people who live close to the Earth say that she is currently deciding whether she has had enough of us. From a perspective that sees humans as cells in the planetary nervous system, it is obvious that we are creating craziness.

The methods developed by the Human Potential Movement in the 1960s and 70s have spread to a lot of people; many of them probably do not even know about the origins of these methods. Personal-development workshops, self-help groups, and so on, are much more accepted now. The time has come, however, when ways are also needed to help move people from personal to planetary awareness—a move towards expansion of consciousness as it relates not just to ourselves, but to those with whom we share the planet—human and non-human.

Evolution entails transcending the boundaries of the self —at least, the self in its current version. For this to happen it is not enough to gain cathartic release by bashing Mum or Dad on a cushion. Neither is it necessarily useful to fixate on "growth", the "spiritual", or affirming our "needs", if these merely serve to maintain the ultimately self-destructive patterns of our egos.

If it is true that the Earth is in "decision time", it is possible that she may also be trying to communicate with us. Part of this communication takes the familiar form of "look at what a mess you're making". The medium for this communication is energy in the form of economic, social, political and ecological stasis. These are manifestations of energy easily recognized because they are material and they affect us in obvious ways: things become scarce or expensive, businesses close, pollution starts to choke us.

Another part of the communication might be "things in yourselves that need attending to". The energy here is harder for us to perceive because it is psychological and spiritual. For most people this is not a perceived need. If we don't feel good, we blame someone else and take another drug. Much personal development work is about showing us how to attend to ourselves. By freeing ourselves from old fears, and gaining clarity, we can begin to empower ourselves to make changes in the areas that seem important. What "seems important", however, is still limited by our perception.

The planet may also be saying: "There are other things you need to attend to. Hear me speak to you directly. Open gates in your minds so that I may speak to you more clearly." But we may not be able to hear, because we may not yet know what we are supposed to be listening to.

Why is it shamans say that "psychologists are merely dabbling in shamanism"? Because in attempting to heal ourselves from our current psychological perspectives we are attending to only a fraction of what influences us.

An experience I had in the early 1980s is a graphic example of this:

I was standing in a misty field in Cornwall at dawn with a circle of people on a Vision Quest. A Medicine Man was berating us for our laziness in seeking our visions and called on powers to help us. I sensed that he was aware of realities we couldn't even guess at. In humility I made a silent vow not to do anything phoney to please him but to be real. Instantly something hit me from the ground up, and I was kicked about eight feet backwards through the air, and knocked unconscious.

When I recovered about twenty minutes later, most of the circle of people had gone. I had so much energy I had to run around the field four times. As I lay on the earth getting my breath back, my life's purpose at this time came to me.

Two years later I asked a shaman about this. "It could be one of three things," he said. (Three?!) "The Whipper, a Thunder Being or your Higher Self. I think it was your Higher Self. When you make a vow with intent, it can turn around and kick you awake."[32]

Spirits, ethereal forms, powers, presences, devas and fairies are obviously nonsense, delusions, and merely figments of a deranged imagination. Any rational person with a well-developed left brain will tell you that. Nevertheless, act "as if" they are really there, and see what happens. Instead of dismissing any phenomena you encounter as purely subjective, allow ambiguity to flourish. Don't chop things off with reason. Give space for the growth of the nebulous and bizarre. Let your right brain breathe. Then after the event, come back to it again with reason.[33]

Methods of communicating range from those using a "tool" as an intermediary, such as a ouija board or dowsing tool, to more directly perceived contact. How easy you find each method will depend on how sensitive you are to the frequencies at which these energies are vibrating.

Set a pendulum swinging and "ask" it to show you what its "yes" is. Note any change of direction, and then repeat for "no", "don't know" and "I won't answer that". Stay relaxed and trust what is happening. A pendulum can be a very useful tool.

Automatic writing is another device that I have found

fruitful. Approach a site with respect, seek permission of its guardian to be there, and ask whatever guidance you want about what seems to be important for you at that time, and then just write whatever comes without censoring.

Although harder to trust, ultimately the most rewarding methods rely on using your own body directly as a channel of communication. The dowsing tool is, after all, only an amplifier of your own bodily response. So tuning in on a frequency that yields more direct information can be more efficient. I'm talking about your inner eye and ear. If you imagine you can see something, don't dismiss it as "merely your imagination". Act "as if" something out there is interacting with your capacity for generating pictures. Maybe it's the only way it can communicate with you. Or, act "as if" your inner voice isn't just you talking to yourself, but something external to yourself activating your capacity for internal speech. Once you begin to trust it, you can use your imagination actively to contact spirit forms. Trust what leaps into your imagination. Trust what it seems to be saying to you and go with it as far as it will take you. Then afterwards, see if it actually makes any sense to you. Allow yourself the experience. Analyse it later.

Treat everything that happens both to you and within your immediate environment as significant—a puff of wind, a crow call, a falling leaf, an itch, a fleeting emotion. Notice what is happening at the periphery of your vision, in the space right at the edge of your visual field where, if you rotated your eyes any further, you would be looking inside your own skull. Curious things happen at the edges between worlds.

It is probably useful to assume that whatever you encounter is an energy field which communicates its essence by stimulating in you the perception of an archetypal form. Fairies may not really be little people with gossamer wings and red hats, but our perception of them that way may correspond most closely to their essence and how they would have us see them. A spriggan might really be nothing more than a knobbly swirl.

Always show respect to beings you encounter. Honour them. Be humble. Don't just bumble into whatever site they may be guarding. Ask them first. Assume you're just a dumb human and they know about other worlds about which you know nothing. They will talk with you if you're polite. On the other hand, they also seem to respond well if you communicate with authority. You can summon spirits and ask them to make their presence felt. But communicating with authority means being genuinely in touch with your own power, being centred, sure of yourself, and coming from the belly. They will know if you're not.

Every sacred site has its guardian spirit. Wells are guarded by slender female spirits about three feet high. Each of the twin wells at Carn Euny has one such spirit, and the well at Sancreed has several. Spirits at wells are often willing to offer advice and healing.

The fogou at Rosemerryn is presided over by three female spirits each about the same size as a human. They are priestesses of some sort, and although their presence is generally benign, they will tolerate no nonsense. They let you know when you're being self-centred or stupid! Spirits at hill forts tend to be imposing and may demand to know what your purpose is and who you are. Bartinney has a guardian spirit which is about fourteen feet tall. Stone circles and hill forts seem to have guardians who initially make their presence felt at the periphery of their respective sites, usually at gateways or obvious entrances.

It is possible to summon some form of spirit almost anywhere in the countryside. The Native Americans stamp their feet and call the little people to bless the site where they intend to stay. You can use little bells, Druids' bells, musical instruments, or simply clap your hands, or use your voice, or intent of will.

Giving your powers of fantasy free reign, you could even talk with a small "imagined" being when out walking. This can be surprisingly beneficial, especially if you talk with it about something that is important for you. Acting "as if" there was actually "something out there", I have occasionally been amazed at the advice I've been given. And what does it matter if I am merely talking to myself, if I happen to be giving myself good advice?

The following are examples of interchanges I've had while using automatic writing. They often have a simplicity and a ring of truth as well as including things that I would not have thought of myself. So, for me at any rate, they have a ring of authenticity.

•

The first is a snippet from an interchange I had with my youngest daughter — we were both attending a workshop run by Jessica Macbeth on communicating with Devas. Emily (aged seven at that time) and I were outside "acting as if" we were "talking" (using automatic writing) to a nature spirit.

(In all that follows, "channelled" material is in italics.)

Emily: "Have you got wings?"

Deva: *"She wants to see me and believe. Tell her I have wings and pointed ears and a smile with bright blue eyes, a small coat with a hood and a back-pack in which I gather herbs to heal and balance."*

Emily: "Have you got spells?"

Deva: *"Tell her I can heal sick plants and animals. I blow in their ears—perhaps this is a spell."*

Emily: "Invisible spells?"

Deva: *"Yes … Love … "*

•

The second was with the guardian of the well at the Sanctuary, near St Buryan:

"It has been a long time since man was here to honour me. Only the cows come. I thank you for remembering me and this place. … Men lived here many years ago. They held this place sacred because of the waters. … This water purifies. There

*are rich veins in my body and my blood flows pure to wash
the valleys … feed my beings … give life to my lushness. The
blood that was here is washed away by me. I restore the peace
and balance to the works of men that have destroyed. Now is
the time when mankind must feel me in their bones and
flesh. You need me to wash through you.*"[34]

•

Late one summer evening as twilight approached, I was sitting
in the garden making notes. Looking up for a moment, I
"saw", with my inner eye, four young women dressed in
flowing white. One of them was slightly separated from the
rest, inclining at an angle to her left and gazing back at me. As I
studied her, inwardly so to speak, something resonated between
us and she beckoned to me. She then leaned back towards the
others, laughing.

I decided, as an experiment, to follow wherever it might
be that "they" wanted to lead me. I would do so with the
innocence of a child, trusting in my imagination, however
naive or peculiar that might seem.

They led me straight to the fogou, where they invited me
to sit outside and wait. They went inside, gathering together
near the mouth of the passage, looking back at me, laughing
and whispering to each other. Then they disappeared and a
mist formed across the entrance.

Another figure appeared at the entrance. This one
produced in me a feeling of respect or awe. The mist took on
the shape of a female form, but when I tried to see clearer
nothing appeared.

This all seemed rather bizarre, and I began to feel uncomfortable. Whatever was there was beckoning or pulling me into
the fogou. It was dark by now, and feeling nervous, I went and
got a torch.

"Why are you afraid?"
"I'm afraid to reach out." The words just came to
me. I had no idea what I meant by them.

"What stops you?"

Again, spontaneously, "I'll be hurt."

"How will you be hurt?"

"There will be nobody there."

"Who will not be there?"

"She will not be there."

"It is your mother you fear. You must face it. You fear the dark. You fear the unknown. All things come from the mother. Put out your light and face your fear. We are here to help you grow strong. Do this."

This is crazy, I thought, standing in the fogou's main passage, but I'll do it.

I switched off the torch and put it on the ground half-expecting a vampire bat to spring out of the dark and clamp its teeth to my neck. But the dark grew gently, softening the edge of my panic. I resumed my breathing, waiting for more voices.

"Now go into the dark."

"I'm already in it."

"Do not be the fool with us. Go now where it is darkest. Face it."

I shuffled forwards, feeling my way along the walls into the darkest part of the passage. Fear cramped my arms from reaching out to touch the wet, cob-webbed stones, fear of spiders and crawling things, fear of the roof caving in, fear of hands that would spring from the cracks and pull me in, fear of the thing that would leap at me with a scream. But there was only wet rock, dead leaves and silence.

"Reach down to your right. There is a gift."

Fumbling in the dark I found a small rock.

"Hold it in your right hand and then in your left. Swing it in each hand and see what it tells you."

I followed the instructions circling each arm in turn against the weight of the rock. When it was in my right hand I felt a sense of my strength and outgoing-ness. When I held it in my left hand I felt strangely open and receptive. Both felt clumsy, yet as I changed the rock from one side to the other the different feelings were unmistakable .

"*How is your fear?*"

"It is gone."

"*This is a first step. Now you must begin to find your balance. Learn to be strong and open. This is the way.*"

I felt around for my torch and, failing to locate it, panicked, frantically sweeping the ground, grabbing for the safety of light. It was nowhere.

I caught himself in mid-flight, stopped scrabbling, and rested on the ground, leaning on my left hand, my right hand closing around the gift-rock for reassurance. I felt the ground's solidity and drew comfort from it, then began a systematic sweep left and right in slow, broad arcs. My hand touched rubber. I paused.

"Thank you ... " and I snapped on the light.

•

Another time, I sat in the main passage with a notepad and pen, just writing whatever came ...

"Who are you?" I asked silently.

"*We are the keepers of this place for all time that this place will be.*"

"Why can't I see you?"

"*You hear us inside you where we talk with you. This is easy for you because you talk much inside you. You need to find the way to see inside you. Then you can see us.*"

"Why should I do this?"

"*Because it is in you to be strong. It is in everyone to be strong. You can help this. It is needed for the changes. Do not doubt this.*"

"What changes?"

"*We cannot see too clearly very far ahead. But this we know. There will be big changes in the way the world is seen by you and others. The things you see around you now will*" *be different. The towns and cities especially: they will be different. But even the countryside: that will be different because there are many things that live here that are dying now. The animals and some of the plants — especially the trees. Look, you can see that there are many of these big creatures that are dead as they stand. And your people do not think much of this. They do not see that these things give them life. That their lives depend on these things."*

"Tell me more about the cities."

"There will not be enough food for all. There will be many who will steal and life will become very dangerous. Others will die inside from sickness of the heart. They will think that there is no longer any point in living because they will think that they have lost too much and so they will just give up. There will be no order because too many will be fighting against the natural order and the forces that your world makes to keep itself in order will no longer be enough. Indeed the more strong those forces are made to keep the order, the more there will be those that will fight against them. And so life will become very difficult.

"But these are not the main changes. The things you will see, which will make the changes seem so great, will be that you will see much more than what you see now. Other worlds will be seen by those who are ready and who wish to see. The world you see now, that you think is so bright, is only the edge of the world as it is. Beyond that edge is so much more to be seen, and little do you know of it. We are a part of that other world that can be seen. But more, much more, than just the voices and beings and spirits and powers that you do not see, are the powers and spirits that you do not see inside yourselves, so much so that you cringe even that such things might be, and laugh them away as so much nonsense and embarrassing rubbish ... "

•

I was sitting having coffee outside the grouproom during a visiting group's intensive workshop. There was a lot of cathartic work going on. Increasingly I felt as if "stuff" was coming out of the grouproom and sticking to me, so I moved to sit outside the fogou. It felt even worse there, like a sewer. After the group had gone, I realized that clearing up had to involve more than hoovering and that the fogou was in some way drawing energy into it but that it was festering. I also remembered reading somewhere about stakes being used to divert energy flow in the landscape. So I collected some iron tubing and set up a line of stakes from the fogou down to the stream, with the intention of drawing the energy out of the fogou and away to flowing water. It worked.

> *Here is what you must do to preserve the purity of Rosemerryn: come here when you can and speak to us of what you feel to be happening. If it gets sick, put out the stakes to drain away to the stream as you did before. Best not to put one in front of the fogou.*
>
> *Talk to us and ask us for help. That is what we are here for. We can intervene too. If necessary we can be posted in the house too. Take us there. We can clear it.*
>
> *Bring David and Judy here on Sunday. Link. Join. Ask them to speak with us in the creep.*

On Sunday at dusk we linked in the main passage. David started singing and Judy and I joined in. Then we went into the creep. In my imagination I "saw" three nature spirits and a woman in white. Their presence was very strong and accompanied, outside, by an owl's hoot and a crow's call. The woman in white enveloped David in a white cloak, strewed him with flowers, and then poured honey over him. She then moved to Judy. An opening appeared in the top of Judy's head, like a vagina, and the woman in white seemed to be assisting Judy in giving birth to something through her head.

We walked the perimeter of the estate. There was a ring around the moon that night. David said he experienced a feeling of great love being showered on him. Judy had a similar feeling and also felt that we should do a sweat lodge soon for healing and cleansing together—which we did.

•

On the recommendation of two visiting medicine women from California, I spent a night in the main passage of the fogou. A crystal altar had been set up earlier in the main passage consisting of some forty or fifty quartz crystals and a central arrangement of large crystal balls. I lay in front of this altar with a candle, torch and a small portable computer. I had intended to leave a candle burning because I was a little nervous about a bat which lives in the main passage.

Tonight you will sleep well and dream, and you must record everything that happens while you sleep. We are all around you always—even when you do not attend to us. The knowledge that we have to give to you is being fed to you all the time but you do not listen. You must listen more carefully ...

Encoded in these walls is all that we knew, for we left it here. Now it is in these crystals—and in your crystal too. You may draw on this if you tune into it.

Feel the silence descending. You are entering another time. Trust it. We are enveloping you ...

You must sleep in the darkness. For lights will come to you. You will remember everything and then may record as soon as you wake, or if you need to, you may light your lamp to do so in the night. Record everything we give you.

Feel the peace in your stomach. This we give to you; this is a sign to you that we care for you. Do not expect what you will receive ...

What do you want to show me?

How to be yourself. Without fear. This lies in your belly. That is where your peace is ...

You seem very big.

We are filling the passage with our presence for you.

I can feel your femininity, your womanness. I can

feel you and hear you but not see you.

Would you like to see us?

Yes, but I am a little afraid of that. This way I can cope.

We do not wish to scare you.

Let me see you just a bit, then. ... When I try to see you in the crystals you seem to have a different face in each crystal — in the west you are very old. In the east you are a virginal face; in the north a round face of a rather nice woman. This is only an impression. The old woman is the most obvious because of the wrinkled brow. The entire crystal is misty, but I imagine there is a shape of a whole woman there, and you seem to move ...

I have doubts about whether or not I am simply fantasizing all this.

When you question us as to whether we exist or not we get angry as we have always done. If I was to materialize here in front of you would freak out — yes, I know your language by now. And I do not wish to frighten you. We can speak very well like this.

A stabbing pain in my belly.

The sensation you have in your belly when I get angry, the contraction, is surely sign enough. We can communicate through your inner ear and through your bodily sensations. This is perfectly adequate. Vision would overload you and probably make you a little crazy, which is why you only for now see us very mistily as a presence.

Go to sleep now, Jo, and we will communicate in your dreams.

I have a sense of you smiling and waving.

That is right. Night-night.

A voice says *"through time, through time"*. Then I have the clear feeling that she is lying beside me. I feel as if I'm spiralling down a black well, going back through time with lots of images. Witchcraft, barrels rolling and clumping into the passage, and horses steaming. Then a lot of people in the passage. No trees, huts outside. An encampment or settlement. Children being in here, lots of them and laughter. A kind of play with the old people in the clan performing. Then small groups of twos or threes receiving teaching. Then fire outside the entrance and a warrior figure with a sword or axe. Threat. They all leave but something is left here with a lot of sound. That is how they encoded. Mass chanting or drumming, bell-like instruments. She wants me to turn out the light and let her lie with me again.

What is your name?

Morwena ... morwen amor wen ... Let me lie with you and show you the way to the star people. This is what we taught. They lay in here and we showed them where they had come from and where they would go back to — so that they knew they must lead right lives and be strong and purposeful, because this is their school. This they knew and we taught them. This was very important. Go to sleep now. I want to fill you with more of my knowledge through your images and dreams.

Just at the point of dawn as light was beginning to break, I saw thin spiral filaments swirling in front of my eyes and around the main capping lintels of the passage. At first I thought this was a retinal image (much like "floaters" or dead cells on the eyeball). But I had never experienced any such spiral phenomena before and they seemed to be moving independently of my eye movements. They most closely resembled the whorls on fingertips, but lots of them, interlaced and moving gently.

Then, suddenly, they burst into hundreds of tiny pricks of light, like stars, moving gently, with the occasional streak as if some of them were shooting stars.

I checked that this was not some kind of self-produced effect by switching my gaze back to the emerging light at the entrance of the fogou, and then redirecting my gaze to several points within the passage. The stars returned unmistakably. The whole passage appeared to be filled with what can best be described as a "star soup" which flowed in and around the stones.

Somehow, I "knew" that what I was seeing was energy, which, although subtle, was clearly "there". These were also the lights which "they" had wanted me to see.[35]

A couple of years later while on holiday in Brittany, I visited the granite chamber of Gavrinis. The spiral carvings on the megaliths were virtually identical to the shapes I had seen in the fogou.

Carved stone at Gavrinis

•

Another time I lit candles in my room, and waited with the keyboard. ... They are in here. Waiting to communicate with me.

May we get in now, Jo? ... The crystal behind you—bring it here and set it beside the computer ...

I see it glow a little like a switched-off TV tube. A face appears. It is a man with a white beard and bushy eyebrows.

Look at the light. ... This is how we recorded. What you see and hear now is a recording.

I have something to say to you who sees me. It concerns the operation of this piece of land, this ring of power. It must be closed and kept closed, not invaded by lines from outside. From up the hill where the women's circle is, it must not be invaded. There will be blood spilled here by the men on the hill who will come over the horizon. There will be very many of them. It must not be invaded here — this must be preserved.

So I have told all who are here. So I have asked that the elders consider the merits of leaving—and the power will be preserved. You who are hearing or seeing this are from a time when these things will be understood again. You will have realized how to read this stone and what we leave here. You will feel the energy as it flows down the hill and you will be ready to work with it and help the people to become strong. If this were not so, you would not be reading this that I am saying. Scrying. That is the word.

(The word "scrying" is significant. It was a word I had heard but did not know the meaning of. When I looked it up in the dictionary it was, of course, totally appropriate in this context.)

I walk here and some have seen me. I have not appeared to you. I am the one who can tell you what happened.

I am a recording. I cannot speak with you. I have put this intent into this place and you are scrying it.

You are sad. You are all sad. This must be so because you will have lost touch with the ways of the people who were here before you. I see this already happening. The men are striving to achieve in the world and they are losing the sight, they are losing the vision and they are losing their souls. The women bemoan this.

I have left this recording so that you may be helped to overcome the fear which you carry. There are ways that this can be done in this place. One such way is to be still in the fogou. To be very still and listen to the sounds of the silence, to the voices that are left here, or will be left here by myself and especially by the women. They will remain. Their voices and presences will remain. This has already been arranged. So come here, be still and listen to them well.

The other thing that you may do is listen to me when I say that there are ways in which you can reverse the process *which will surely have happened when you will have become so separated from your true purpose. You will find your own ways, I am sure. This is the teaching which has been passed down for many hundreds of years which the elders and the wise ones have striven to communicate to those that have been chosen to receive it. I do not know what ways you will use; I know only that there will be such ways.*

Our ways no longer will be appropriate for you. To do battle in such a way that the body and mind are perfectly aligned may not be your way. I cannot see that far ahead. But I am sure that you will need to find some way to align the mind and body, for this is the aspect of the balance which is a mirror of the balance in Nature and in the relationship between men and women. This is what is beginning to go out of alignment, when the men are becoming carried away with their power and the women must go underground. So I would say look to your mind and body — though I do not know how.

Also look to the heavenly mind and the earthly body and how these are joined. Again, use your ways. By your time, our ways will seem primitive. They are, after all, befitting only the people of this time. Your time will be different.

We shall be leaving here and these things will be left in the walls of the stones so that you may scry them. There will be more, is more. It is programmed for you to scry it when you are ready to receive. You will be able to receive only what you are ready to receive.

The heart of man is the doorway to the stars. When this is open he can not only read the mind of others and travel where he will, he can create whatever his heart desires. The women here still know this, but it is losing to the desires of the men to vanquish through power, through the power which comes from their bellies. Yes, they are dropping down into the world of the material, which pleases them. The women are still in touch with the higher planes of being through the openness of their hearts, which the men are losing.

A long time ago it was different. We are all descending. It is sad. We are coming out of the mists of creation when all was one. We are separating. I suppose this must be, so that we may discover who we are and what me must do—although often I regret that this must be.

The women will get dragged down to the plane of the belly because there is much power in the material world and in its delights. Their finer tuning will linger for a long while, but I doubt not that it will be vanquished by those that will decry it as belonging to times that are past and must go. It is sad.

You who are scrying this will know that things must be restored to their natural balance. If this were not so you would not be scrying this.

I cannot see into the times ahead. I do not know how it will be or what will have become of the people. This much I can see: that this process will grow faster because it is like a drug that will catch at the minds of the people. There are too many attractions in descending into matter. It satisfies the baser desires and the body. That will be too hard to resist. And in that will come separation. This must be—separation from the heart, separation from the spirit and soul. Separation between men and women. Separation between the old and new. And separation from the source of all things and true knowledge of who we are. I can see no other possible way but this.

And this is my only purpose in leaving this here and these voices, that you who hear them now, may be inspired by these recordings. If what I say rings true for you and you can understand me, then the messages and teachings which I will be leaving here must be sent out so that the most people may hear them and be moved to change from these ways that I see. I do not know any other way.

Take the Crystal.

I place it to my forehead. I see green fields and hills ... Yellow ... Light ... White Light growing stronger. A figure emerging as if in a mist. A man with robes. He holds something in his right hand. It is glowing. He seems to be writing. That's not possible. They didn't write. He looks up at me. He smiles. It is for me to write? He nods and smiles. I can feel a veil closing around my body. There is a growing silence in the room, a wave of peace.

Receive. Receive. … Let me put my hand on your heart. So gently. Subtly. I do not wish to frighten you as before when I, or my sisters, held your head.

I am instructed to look up, roll my eyes upwards. I feel a rush of energy coming down from the crystal on my head. And then an image of the Priestess, Morwena: she is in silver white and beautiful. She is about halfway down the fogou.

Take the crystal in your left hand. Remove your watch and your glasses.

I wish to see you.

If you do it will make you crazy, Jo. You will get lost in your fantasy. Best that you just write what I speak to you. This is the way we can be with each other. It is more comfortable for you and for me because I do not have to be concerned about frightening you.

What do you wish to say to me?

Can you really hear me?

How do you mean?

Do you believe this is my voice and not yours?

I am not sure.

I know. How can I tell you what I have to say to you if I cannot be sure that you are hearing me?

I believe you are there and trying to speak with me.

Very well then. Write this: The power of this place must now be released through the fogou. Strong ceremony must be worked here for the people. Gather those who work for you and guide them to make a focused vision. This must be the vision: Healing. Find what it is you bring as healers and send that out. Meld it into one vision—a strong one—and project it mightily. The people will catch it, for it is needed. Attend more to my land. It is being neglected. Find your love, your heart, and all else will follow. ... Yes, we are watching this place closely and all the people. We are coming to those who would heal. This is all you must do. There is no great secret. Send out the healing power and it will attract what is needed. It must be ... "broadcast".

Thank you for letting me use your words from your mind, Jo. "Broadcast" is the good word. It travels on the etheric.

•

A workshop I want to run is not filling. I remember the message from the fogou about "broadcasting" and decide to do a ceremony to "send out" what the workshop has to offer. I light candles in the fogou, arrange flowers, incense and a copy of the brochure for the group. I sit meditating on what I have to offer and why I want more people, not for personal gain, but because some good might come of it for the people. I explain that I need two more for the workshop to be viable.

As I leave the fogou I can hear the telephone ringing. It is a booking. The next day there is another booking. The workshop runs. One of the participants says: "Something made me just want to come ... I felt pulled."

•

I often use a "fogou initiation" with groups, a ceremony which has evolved over the years into its present form. The intention of the ceremony is to create conditions in which people can become more attuned to Mother Earth. Part of the process of the ceremony involves some disorientation in order to bypass a "normal" state of consciousness. The end of the ceremony includes an attempt to communicate with the "Little People" in the fogou and to pass on any messages they may have for individuals in the group. To do this at all I have to suspend disbelief. I just have to say whatever comes, without censoring.

I find it also helps to disguise my voice and talk "as if" I were a pixie, gnome or whatever. It is also more fun that way.

The group divides in two and one half is blindfolded. The blindfolded half help each other into the depths of the fogou and through the pool of water, which is usually present, where they wait for a pre-arranged signal. Then one by one they feel their way, alone and still blindfolded, up the passage of the fogou and into the "creep". Rattles and drumming accompany their journey. Once in the creep they squat, waiting. In a short while the partner from the other half of the group leads the person, still blindfolded, on an exploration of the land with its smells, textures, tastes, sensations and sounds.

Meanwhile, I dress the fogou with crystals, incense and about one hundred candles. After everyone has done the "blind walk", an assistant and I lead them in a line, holding hands and still blindfolded, into the main passage, where they wait.

I take up a position near the edge of the pool, squatting or sitting on a low stool. I wear something with a hood so that I can't see or identify the members of the group. Focusing my attention on the ground by my feet, I summon the "Little People" with a Druid bell—a silver ball with chimes, which I roll in the palm of my hand.

The assistant leads the people one by one to the edge of the pool and invites them to hold a question in mind or make a wish. At this point the Little People usually have something to say, so I communicate it. Words just tumble out, almost always in the form of a riddle. As far as I am concerned, it could be gibberish. I find that it is important not to know who the person is that I am talking to, otherwise I might colour the message with my own ideas or projections, or just feel inhibited. (I occasionally do this for someone else's group, so that I really do not know anything about the people anyway. In any event, I generally do this ceremony on the first day of a workshop before I get to know people.) When the message ends, the assistant removes the person's blindfold, and I can usually hear a gasp as they take in the beauty of the candles and crystals reflected in the pool. The overall effect is stunningly magical.

Recently I have been recording these "messages" on a cassette-recorder and transcribing them. I then give a copy to individuals and invite their comments, stressing that it might be garbage and I don't mind if they say so. I am consistently surprised as to how relevant these riddles from the Little People seem to be. Here are a few examples, together with comments from the people concerned.

> *Here is one who dances in a ring with the little people. They wear robes of pink and green. For they too understand that we live in the edge between the worlds where this one too can see. For this one has sparkles behind the eyes that connect them to the unseen, for they can see the world of the unseen and the interior. Hmm ... They should do this more often.*

> "I have been for ten years on a search into the unseen and I give courses in that ... I am also working through travelling around the world to connect the stars with the earth by meditation and work with the land where I am—America, Europe, Mongolia, Russia, Australia. It is the unseen of the cosmos."

> *Now we think that this one comes with silver armour that protects them from the sharp points of those that wear rags. For this one walks with a kind of a step which is more like a dance, which is very peculiar — because they wear armour. How can they dance when they wear such armour? Ah ... because it is thin, silvery, elfin-like. So it can be removed with ease.*

> "This feels appropriate to my natural ability to switch from one state or emotion to another very quickly. It also tells me that my defences aren't as rigid and restricting as I tend to think they are ... "

> *Here comes one who rides on swans' backs across deep waters, trailing fish-hooks to catch those that cannot swim. For this one too has a magical nature that can entice people across the*

worlds so that they may learn to let go of their wounds.

"I can connect this with my daily therapy work in the hospital. ... Many times I have to cry when people tell me about their wounds ... "

Something unexpected often happens when there are no more people to give messages to, particularly when I think there still are. On one occasion the Druid's bell jumped out of my hand. Or I will get a message that "that's it" even when I am sure there are more. I once kept count of the group and knew there was another person. The Little People insisted there wasn't and no other message came. It later turned out that the "missing person" had been meditating in the far end of the creep and was unavailable for messages.

Tree spirit (Hunt, 1871)

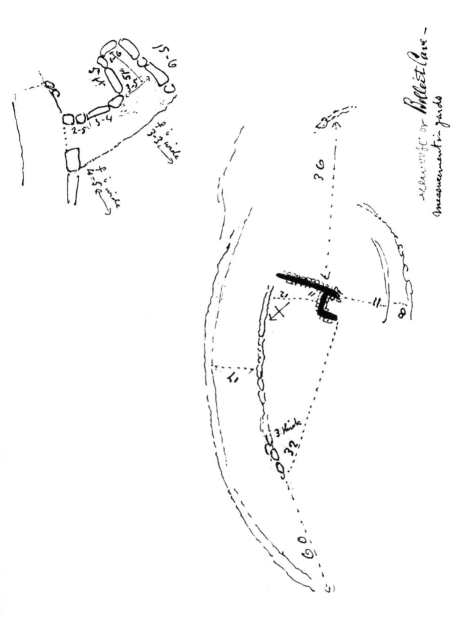

Fogou ("Bolleit Cave") and bank, measurements in yards (Blight, 1864)

13

Hidden Chambers

Several references indicate that at one time the fogou may have been more extensive than it is now. Hals in 1702, speculating on the fogou, said:

> How far it extends no man now living can tell ... for as soon as you go an arrow's flight, or less, into it, your candles will ... be extinguished for want of air.[36]

Was this just fancy? An arrow's flight is a long way. Borlase in 1754 noticed that

> at the end fronting the entrance, there is another square hole, within which there was also a further vault now stopped up with stones, through which you see the light; and therefore I doubt not but here was a passage for light and air, if not a back way of conveying things into and out of these cells ... [37]

In 1871, a member of the Royal Institution of Cornwall on an excursion to the fogou was reported as noting that:

> the bank just opposite the branch cavern sounded hollow, from which he is persuaded that there is a chamber underneath to be yet explored.[38]

Blight reported that "diverging fences suggested that other cavities and chambers subterranean probably existed in the immediate neighbourhood."[39]

Several accounts suggest that the fogou "was formerly regarded with superstitious awe and was believed to be of incredible extent."[40] Others describe witches being pursued through the fogou "for a mile or more".[41]

> There is a tradition, firmly believed on the lower side of Burian, that the Fugoe Hole extends from the cliffs underground so far that the end of it is under the parlour of Trove. ... A pool of water some distance from the entrance prevents any adventurer from exploring the Hole to its termination. Hares often take refuge in the Fugoe Hole, from which they have never been known to return.[42]

A large stone blocks a doorway at the end of the creep. This was excavated in the late 1940s by Evelyn Clark and Dr Ford:

> A trench, 4 foot 10 inches in length and 2 foot 2 inches wide, was dug across the back of the blocking stone. ... The rab continued to rise, but more steeply, to a step 10 inches above the inner face of the stone. ... The walls suggest a continuation of the passage, but no real indication that they ever extended further is evident, the step and the steep rise in ground level precluding the further extension of the creep. The opening, which the blocking stone fills, was later found to have been a constructed doorway.[43]

If it is a doorway, then what is it a doorway to?

An Ordnance Survey map of 1877 shows the site before the present house was built. The creep passage on this map seems to be about ten times its present length and about three times the size of the main fogou passage. It is also shown to extend beyond the boundary of the innermost rampart of the fort. Evelyn Clark considered this map to be incorrect.

Ian Cooke, author of the definitive work on fogous, suggests that "this odd feature could represent a path crossing rough ground to the fogou".[44] This seems the most likely explanation, but, given that the map may be inaccurate, there is

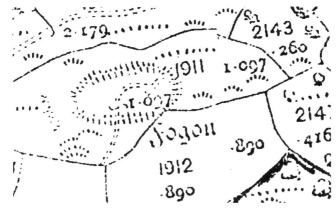

OS map, 1877

also some difficulty with it.

I scanned images of the 1877 map and a more recent one (both 25 inches to the mile) into my computer, and then matched and superimposed the images. The siting of the fort ramparts on the older map bears a questionable relationship to what is actually on the ground. In places there seems to be discrepancy of between ten and twenty feet. In relation to a

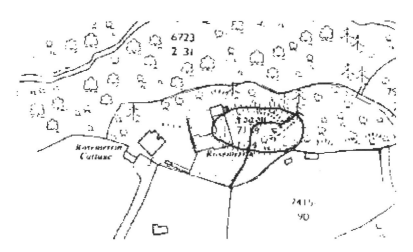

Current OS map with 1877 fort outline superimposed. This coincides with Time Team's findings.

109

possible extended creep passage (or path), this is critical. A five-foot error means the difference between a "path" on the map leading apparently nowhere and one ending in a ten-foot drop right by some interesting stonework which resembles a grotto.

During the three-day workshop in 1987 that I mentioned earlier, the Métis Cherokee shaman told me that there is another chamber — an "antechamber" — attached to the fogou and that it was time to open it. During the search for the antechamber we should allow no photographs in the fogou until the excavation is finished.

"When the ancestors want us to take advantage of power spots, they sing power songs," the shaman said. "Photos can interfere with this — it fixes the energy. Many spirits work with the excavators. If they don't want it done, the excavators will die."

He also said I should not allow anyone else to run ceremonies as part of the "opening". Presumably he meant that as guardian of the site, I should commune with the spirits about what is going on.

This made sense to me. Before I came, the site had developed the reputation for a having a curse on it because the original owners had demolished most of it to build a house. I doubted if the spirits were consulted. Any further interference would need to be respectful. As indicated next, disturbing the site can have some odd consequences.

Thumping on the lawn in front of the house and in an area near the fogou produces a resonant sound which suggests that something lies underneath. I spent an hour stamping around with members of the Cornwall Archaeology Unit, and they agreed.

I dowsed a likely area and got a strong response from the rods. I then probed the lawn, appropriately I thought, with a replica Celtic sword, struck rock, and dug a trial trench. I found seven regular-shaped stones which seemed to have been placed by man rather than Nature.[45]

As things often seem to go here, someone visited during my dig who just happened to be an archaeologist and just happened to have his trowel on him. He said that the stones were almost certainly part of the base of an Iron Age hut. Carefully slicing the edges of the trench with his trowel he revealed black crumbs which he said were pieces of Iron Age pottery. He reckoned this was possibly one of the most exciting unexcavated sites in the south of Britain. I was thrilled, even though I had not found any more of the fogou.

Then I realized that I had not specified what I was dowsing for. I had simply "asked" the rods to find something—anything. And they had.

I left the trench open for a couple of weeks while wondering how to proceed. During this time people staying at the centre fell ill. Then we had a workshop and someone got quite disturbed because they said that the previous night they had seen a hessian-clad foot sliding along the floor of their bedroom. Others sharing the room also claimed to have heard it shuffling.

I added "deal with hessian-clad foot" to my list of household chores, exorcized it, and filled in the trench. No more problems.

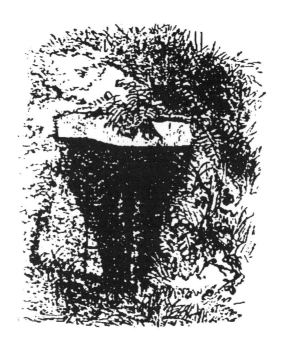

Fogou entrance (Blight)

14

*D*eath and Rebirth

The recession bit hard in the autumn of 1993 and the centre lost a lot of groups. This came at a time when I was undergoing a profound internal shift anyway. So I found myself struggling to hold on to my external world, while at the same time needing to let go inside.

In the depths of my internal questioning when I wondered if I and the centre were going through death into rebirth, or just into death, a baby was born here.

David and Judy had separated and gone their independent ways a few years previously. Judy teamed up with a visiting shaman, and went to live in Arizona. She returned for many years bringing teachings and wisdom from the Native American tradition. Just before he left, David was told by the fogou that he was being "prepared" and would have another wife and, this time, a child. Later, he married Julie, at Rosemerryn.

The place, too, honoured the deaths in his life. Rosie, David's dog, was buried near the fogou, and one moonlit night Julie miscarried, squatting over a little pit ringed with flowers.

On the day she learned she was pregnant again, Julie told the fogou and this time felt blessed. Six weeks before their baby was due, Julie and David stayed at Rosemerryn to look after the place during a workshop while I was away. To remember Rosie, who had died exactly a year and a day previously, they went into the fogou. Julie felt a tug on her womb as if the fogou was physically stimulating the onset of labour, triggering birth. Joseph was born that night.

David was amazed at the speed of it. An hour after the

birth, he returned to the fogou.

"I was totally gob-smacked by the whole thing. It was only in the fogou that I actually realized what had happened. That was where I went to kind of take a breath, to mark the event. And it was there, on an emotional level, that it really struck home in my body, struck home in my heart."

The fogou had pulled him. David had been married twice at Rosemerryn, and although he had not chosen it to be where he would become a father, the place had.

In the synchronous way that events happen here, the workshop during which Joseph was born was called "Homecoming—healing the inner child".

Not yet ready to accept such a positive sign of rebirth, I sought guidance in the fogou. After all, maybe the spirits wanted me to move on and have someone else in — my "death" for another "birth". "Please give me a sign," I asked. "Make it obvious, but gentle. No trees falling on my head, thanks." After meditating silently for a while, an inner voice told me to open my eyes. In the wavering candlelight, I saw the unmistakable face of an old woman nodding at me from the shadows in the stones.

A year later ...

The soft glow of candlelight greets me as I pick my way through the trees. A visiting group has been doing a ceremony, but the fogou is now empty, except for a candle burning at the far end. It is midnight. A pair of owls call to each other.

Outside the entrance I tell the fogou how I am feeling weary and despairing. I don't see how I can stay at the centre any more. Recalling the shaman's words about opening up concealed parts of the fogou, I had offered a four-day workshop in CAER's programme called "Hidden Chambers". I felt this would be a good way to gather people to help me with the task, and would also attract people to the centre. But there are not enough takers and I have to cancel. I feel crushed.

When I started the centre sixteen years previously, I

resolved to stay as long as it worked. Now it is looking as though I may soon have to leave.

A wind gusts and swirls around the trees, chilling me. I am ushered through the entrance. The guardians of the fogou seem welcoming. I tell them my troubles and they listen. I say how I find it hard to believe them any more when the signs go against any sense of things improving.

The candle at the far end of the passage flickers. It looks as if it will go out. I think that this is probably a sign that I'm going to have to go too. Then the candle pulses into life and glows steadily. It does this several times.

A voice urges me to write, to continue with this book, started twelve years previously. One of the guardians insists I complete it "this month". It is the 25th. That's absurd. It gives me only five days.

"One month to the next full moon," comes the reply.

That gives me three weeks. I start writing. I don't know how it will improve anything, but it feels better to be channelling my energy creatively.

While writing, I get a telephone call from someone who visited earlier in the summer curious about the Hidden Chambers workshop. He is the producer of *Time Team*, an archaeological programme on Channel Four Television, and he wants to do a piece on the fogou. *Time Team* uses ground-probing radar, computers linked to satellites, and geophysics which produces images of what lies underground. He says they want to map the site and explore the possibility of a hidden chamber.

We fix dates for filming.

The fogou has a mind of its own. It is home to an energy which is conscious, a domain for occupants of an "other reality". They want to reveal their secrets. They want to communicate and be heard. Most of the time I do not listen, am too down-to-earth, busy, stubborn or ill-equipped. Nevertheless, I am moved to mount a workshop, which attracts, not participants, but a TV producer with access to equipment which can probe the earth in a manner that is non-intrusive. I could never have imagined that the fogou might one day be explored through the medium of Virtual Reality.

Inside the damp, slabbed, granite passage lie secrets waiting to be tapped. These are not secrets that will manifest as something "out there". They are keys to finding something within ourselves, buried aspects of our own psyches, untapped powers and potentials.

Listen and the fogou stirs ancient memories, forgotten dreams.

You want my secrets, she says, *you want to find more of me? You want the ancient songs of knowledge encoded in my stones?*

Then listen, not to me, but to yourselves ...

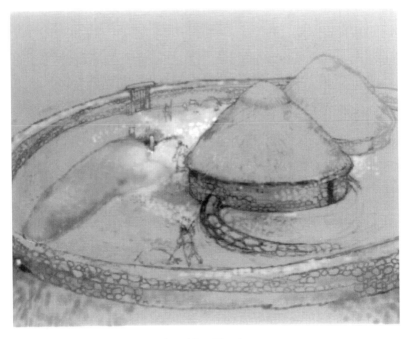

Impression of the site (Victor Ambrus, Time Team)

fterword

Time Team arrived at the end of March 1995. The site was invaded, with military precision, by over sixty people including TV crew, archaeologists, researchers, computer operators and presenters, along with cameras, lights, walkie-talkies, computers, a sixty-foot crane and a helicopter. Hidden chambers, I thought, wouldn't stand a chance.

Within an hour of arriving, a geophysics team had laid out an electronic grid on the lawn and produced a computer

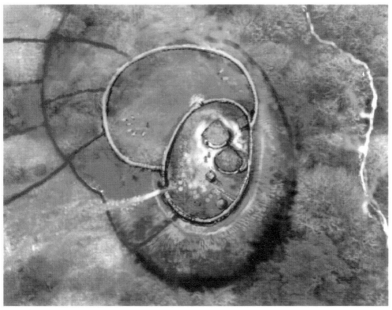

Aerial impression of the site (Victor Ambrus, Time Team)

printout of what lay underneath it. The printout showed something resembling a long tunnel curving under the lawn. With excitement the archaeologists dug two trenches and found ... a water pipe. Another trench across a probable rampart nearer the fogou revealed a pile of rubble. At the end the day, it seemed as if the site was remarkable for its archaeological sterility.

That night I had a dream in which the fogou said: "If you want to find more then dig closer to me." Next morning it turned out that that was what the team had decided to do. As they extended their original trench near the fogou, their finds later led them to describe the programme as "fantastic".

Time Team's excavations revealed a section of an Iron Age house enclosed by a single oval defensive wall. Within one of the "rooms" they found over sixty pieces of pottery, virtually all from the early Iron Age, some with patterning, and a quern stone — an implement for grinding corn. They also found Mesolithic flint and some pieces of medieval pottery. It seems

Ian Cooke's impression of the site (after Time Team)

that this has been a desirable spot since the first millennium BC. The Iron Age site is special in that it has room for only one or two houses together with the fogou, which dominates most of one end of the enclosure. This makes the settlement resemble a vicarage and its church, or the local healer or priestess's residence, set apart from, yet serving the local community. *Time Team* concluded that the purpose of the fogou was for the spiritual life of the occupants of the settlement, and that "there was a lot more to these structures than could be explained by conventional archaeology".[46]

Not shown on the TV programme were the findings of a dowser. He said the fogou had originally been built by at least forty women who had cleared the site to ground level and then built up the walls, packing soil back as they built. The lintels, he said, were lifted using skins. He felt that the fogou had been used for healing and as a place to dry out alcoholics, presumably because alcohol, in those days, had been more commonplace than tea.

When the shaman told me that there was a hidden *chamber* waiting to be discovered, and that opening it would

Black glazed pot, computer-reconstructed from shard found at Rosemerryn (Victor Ambrus, Time Team)

release energy, I thought he meant that there was a hidden *passage*. I was wrong.

The excavations revealed no further extension to the fogou. If there is one, it is short because of the ground disturbance when the house was built. Any further passage extends from the creep, where *Time Team* was unable to excavate, because the fogou is a scheduled site.

The hidden chamber which the shaman told me about may refer to the *room* of the Iron Age house. Opening this did indeed release energy, although how that manifested is less obviously tangible than stones and pots.

On the evening of *Time Team*'s departure after everyone had gone, I sat with the open trench. The next day it would be filled in again to preserve it, but now for a short while I was alone in spirit with its former occupants.

I closed my eyes and imagined myself back in those times. Voices and images came. I had sense of myself as a custodian, tending and nursing the place until the time was right for its true purpose to evolve. I was also aware of the protective

More pots reconstructed from finds (Time Team)

function of the site, its original occupants having hidden, perhaps, in the long passage of the fogou when they were raided by hostile neighbours. After all, a church makes a good sanctuary if your attackers hold it sacred too.

My mind wandered a bit, and I found myself asking if there might be a gift for me. So much pottery had been found by the archaeologists and it had all been sent off to Exeter University to be recorded. Part of me wanted to find something myself. I opened my eyes and noticed a rectangular stone in the bottom of the trench. It was a piece of tin ore — the source of the Celts' wealth. I took this as a good omen.

In the days that followed, I resisted entering the fogou. In my personal life, illusions were crumbling. It was as if my association with the fogou was standing in the way of the woman I loved. I felt frustrated and angry. I even dreamed of slicing up the fogou with a sword. Maybe the time had come for me to leave. My psyche was at work.

A short while later I received an e-mail from the Wisdom School in the USA inviting me to participate in a Cyber Ritual to celebrate Earth Day:

Thu, 20 Apr 95 13:13:49 GMT
From: wisdom@digital.net
To: jomay@thenet.co.uk
Subject: Cyber Ritual—let's start with Earth Day

Dear Friends

I propose that we begin world-wide on-line Cyber Rituals. These rituals should facilitate creation of a cyber-community based on shared experiences of soul-awakening.

Let's begin on Earth Day — this Sunday, April 23rd, 1995. At 12 noon your time, take time to meditate, to empty yourself of all thoughts, give positive feelings and love to the Earth, to Gaia, and to open yourself to any messages back from her. Add whatever other personal touches to this basic ritual that you are comfortable with.

The basic idea is to tune into the living entity of Earth, to give to Mother Earth your love, and to open yourself to what She may be trying to tell you. Maybe the message will be in words, maybe in colors, symbols, sounds, feelings, visions ...

Just be quiet—(stop the inner dialogue)—and be open long enough so that you can hear this higher entity, rather than just yourself.

Then to complete the ritual, come back and share with us what happens ...

This was the prompt I needed. At the pre-arranged time, I entered the main passage of the fogou with a candle, a micro-cassette recorder and my replica Iron Age sword—which sort of wanted to come too. I lit the candle, placed it on the floor of the main passage in a small bowl alongside the sword, sat in a "mindfulness posture", spine erect, attending to my breath, shoulders relaxed, and gazed with soft focus on the candle. The fogou was peaceful, warm and welcoming.

After a few moments, as my mind slowed down, I had the sense of being asked to close my eyes, by several female "presences". As I did so, I felt myself to be travelling through some other kind of passage and I was invited to "speak".

I recounted what was happening for me in my personal life to the "presences", and I also said that I had the possibility of putting out a message to the world at large. (It seemed inappropriate to go into the mechanics of the how!)

I then received a message from the presences in the fogou:

> I would speak to those who would listen. We are in times of much danger for the people. There will be those who can make it through the changes and those who cannot. Those that will make it through the changes will be those that can listen to me. That is to say, to listen to your hearts, to listen to your bodies, to trust the wisdom of your bellies and your soul.

For those that are separate from the ways of the Great Mother will harm themselves in harming me. There will need to be much adaptation, letting go of what no longer is appropriate, and embracing the direction that will lead to enlightenment. There is no other way, for it is already in motion. These are things that many know already. These are words that are not new. There are no new messages. The same message can only be repeated until people know it in their hearts, and act. Being still and listening is good. Letting go of the interference of the mind.

Then came a personal message.

This message is for you, Jo. We love you and understand what is happening for you. All things will be well. You do right to stay with your process, as you call it. From what happens now will emerge much that will be good. ... We honour you. We pray for you. But you need not fear as to the outcome. ... When you stood by the house and all was quiet again, you saw how perhaps you are here only as a custodian, holding the energy until others come. But whoever those are, they must step into the power. You have taken as much as you can of your connection to this land. You have operated here to your capacity. It may be that you will leave. ... If you wish, I can release you. ...Yes, think about that.

I felt really cold. Something had gone. The candle was burning dimly.

Before reporting on my ceremony via the Internet, I went down to the fogou again, curious to see if the candle had gone out. It was still burning, which was reassuring. But also something rather extraordinary was happening.

The sun, which does not usually enter the far end of the fogou, had penetrated its darkest recesses, and a bright chink of light was flickering there—just like the flame of a candle.

A caution
Ancient power spots, and sacred sites like fogous, are gateways.
The real openings lie in our own hearts, minds, and lives.

Rosemerryn has been home to CAER — Centre for Alternative Education and Research — since 1978. CAER is a centre for human potential, similar to many other such centres which are emerging around the world, where people can take time out of their lives to learn more about themselves.

As we make the transition from the industrial age into an unknown future, an essential part of the way forward lies in our waking up as human beings — fully functioning, fully feeling, and fully conscious.

We won't go far unless we do.

CAER offers a round-the-year programme of residential workshops and training courses in personal and spiritual development. Further details from:

CAER
Rosemerryn, Lamorna, Penzance, Cornwall, TR19 6BN
Telephone: (01736) 810530
(*International:* +44 1736 81 0530)
Email: jomay@thenet.co.uk
Website: http://www.thenet.co.uk/~jomay

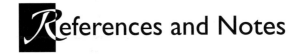eferences and Notes

Apart from the references below, Rosemerryn and its fogou are also mentioned in the following books:
• Shirley Toulson, *The Moors of the South West,* Hutchinson, 1984.
• Craig Weatherhill, *Belerion, Ancient Sites of Land's End,* Alison Hodge, 1981.
• Michael Williams, *Strange Happenings in the Cornish Landscape,* Bossinney Books, 1981.

Television programmes featuring the fogou have included:
• *Landscape of Stone*, BBC2   21 February 1986
• *Pebble Mill at One*, BBC1   2 May 1986
• *Into the Underworld*, TSW   12 April 1990
• *Time Team*, Channel Four Television   7 January 1996

Notes in the text

1 *Map of Southern Britain in the Iron Age,* Ordnance Survey, 1975.
2 Ithell Colquhoun (1906–), *The Living Stones.*
3 W. Hals, *Compleat History of Cornwal, General and Parochial,* manuscript, 1702.
4 Blight, *Churches and Antiquities of West Cornwall*, Parker, London, 1885.
5 William Bottrell, *Traditions and Hearthside Stories of West Cornwall,* Penzance, 1870.
6 *Duffy and the Devil,* in R. Hunt, *Popular Romances of the West of England,* Hotton, 1865.

7   Ian Mcneil Cooke, *Mother and Sun, the Cornish Fogou*, Men-An-Tol Studio, Penzance, 1993, p311.

8   Crosbie Garstin, *The Owls' House*, The Cornish Library, Anthony Mott Ltd., 1982 (first published 1923).

9   Blight, *ibid*.

10 L. Lusk, *The Life and Work of B. W. Leader RA*, 1901.

11 Personal communication from Nic Hale, Garstin's biographer.

12 The "Keigwin" Valley is probably the Lamorna Valley, and "Monks Cove" is Lamorna Cove. There is indeed an angle in the stream which runs from Bartinney Hill, and this is where Rosemerryn is located.

13 Crosbie Garstin, *The Owls' House*.

14 Crosbie Garstin, *China Seas*, Chatto and Windus, 1930.

15 Evelyn Clark, *Cornish Fogous*, Methuen, 1961.

16 John Michell, *The View Over Atlantis*, Sago, London, 1969; *The New View Over Atlantis*, Harper & Row, New York, 1983.

17 Peter Dawkins, *Landscape Temples*, manuscript.

18 Tom Lethbridge, *The Legend of the Sons of God: a fantasy?* Routledge, London, 1972.

19 Alan Bleakley, "The Merry Maidens," *The Ley Hunter*, 1982.

20 David Boadella, *Wilhelm Reich: the evolution of his work*. Vision Press, London, 1973.

21 Don Robbins, *Circles of Silence*, Souvenir Press, 1985.

22 Evelyn Clarke, *ibid*.

23 John Sharkey, *Celtic Mysteries*, Thames and Hudson, 1975. Also personal communication from Paul Potter.

24 Peter Dawkins, Personal communication, 5 October 1981. Peter Dawkins was, together with Sir George Trevelyan, one of the founders of the Gatekeeper Trust, which sponsored journeys to sacred sites worldwide.

25 Jo May, "Living with a Fogou," *Meyn Mamvro*, Issue 3.

26 John Heron, *Cooperative Inquiry into Altered States of Consciousness*, Human Potential Research Project, Department of Educational Studies, University of Surrey, in association with the British Postgraduate Medical Federation, University of London, March 1984. And "Impressions of the Other Reality" in Peter Reason (Ed), *Human Inquiry in Action*,

Developments in New Paradigm Research, Sage, 1988.

27 Cheryl Straffon, "Fogou Experiences," *Meyn Mamvro*, Summer 1989.

28 K.G., "Spirit of the Fogou," *Meyn Mamvro*, Summer 1989.

29 Geraldine Andrew, "Dor Dama," *Meyn Mamvro*, Summer 1992.

30 Eileen Herzberg, "A Visit to the Goddess," *Crann Bethadh*, August 1992.

31 Jo May, "Two-Facedness and Personality Judgements," *Bulletin of the British Psychological Society*, 1978. Also: Peter Stringer and Jo May, "Attributional Asymmetries in the Perception of Moving, Static, Chimeric and Hemisected Faces," *Journal of Nonverbal Behaviour*, Vol 5, No 4, Summer 1981.

32 Jo May, "Awakening," *Self and Society, the European Journal of Humanistic Psychology*, Vol XVIX, No 1, Jan-Feb 1991.

33 John Heron, *Confessions of a Janus Brain*, Endymion Press, 1987.

34 Jo May, "Talking with Spirits," *Meyn Mamvro*, Issue 4.

35 Paul Devereux, *Places of Power*, Blandford, 1990, p165.

36 W. Hals, *Compleat History of Cornwal, General and Parochial,* manuscript, 1702.

37 W. Borlase, *Antiquities Monumental and Historical of the County of Cornwall,* 1754 (EP Publishing, 1973).

38 W. Bottrell, *Traditions and Hearthside Stories of West Cornwall*, Penzance, 1870.

39 V. Russell, manuscript at Royal Institute of Cornwall, from Cooke I, 1993.

40 H. Hencken, *The Archaeology of Cornwall and Scilly*, Methuen, 1932.

41 W. Bottrell, *ibid.*

42 R. Hunt, *Popular Romances of the West of England*, Hotton, London, 1871.

43 E.V. Clark, *Cornish Fogous*, Methuen, 1961.

44 Ian Mcneil Cooke, *Mother and Sun, the Cornish Fogou*, Men-An-Tol Studio, Penzance, 1993.

45 *Time Team*'s excavations confirmed that what I had discovered was part of an Iron Age wall, probably enclosing a small paddock.

46 Tim Taylor, *Time Team 96—The Site Reports*, Channel Four Television.

GOTHIC IMAGE PUBLICATIONS

Gothic Image Publications is a Glastonbury-based imprint dedicated to publishing books and pamphlets that offer a new and radical approach to our perception of ourselves and the world. These are some of our current publications:

The Avalonians
Patrick Benham

Conflict in the Caucasus
Svetlana Chervonnaya

Devas, Fairies and Angels
William Bloom

Dowsing the Crop Circles
edited by John Michell

Dragons: Their History and Symbolism
Janet Hoult

Glastonbury Abbey
James Carley

Glastonbury: Maker of Myths
Frances Howard-Gordon

The Glastonbury Tor Maze
Geoffrey Ashe

The Green Lady and the King of Shadows
Moyra Caldecott

Labyrinths: Ancient Myths and Modern Uses
Sig Lonegren

The Living World of Faery
R J Stewart

Meditation in a Changing World
William Bloom

Needles of Stone Revisited
Tom Graves

The New Ley Hunter's Guide
Paul Devereux

New Light on the Ancient Mystery of Glastonbury
John Michell

Positively Wyrd: Harnessing the Chaos in your Life
Tom Graves

Robin Hood: Green Lord of the Wildwood
John Matthews

Sacred England
John Michell

The Sacred Magician: A Ceremonial Diary
William Bloom

Saint or Satan? The Life and Times of Russia's New Rasputin, Anatoly Kashpirovsky
Galina Vinogradova

Spiritual Dowsing
Sig Lonegren

Symbolic Landscapes: The Dreamtime Earth and Avebury's Open Secret
Paul Devereux

Wyrd Allies
Tom Graves

Gothic Image Publications are available from all good bookshops or direct from

7 High Street • Glastonbury, Somerset • England • BA6 9DP
Telephone +44 1458 83 1453 • (Fax +44 1458 83 1666)